Linda Griffin
about the coi
in so many fa
breaking poin... ...great sensitivity and profound
psychological insight, she deals with issues such as
the value and drawbacks of "time-out" as a remedy
to calm conflict situations, and ways of helping a
child cope after a death in the family. Drawing upon
her long experience as a teacher of the very young,
and to her commitment as a parenting advisor,
Linda Griffin offers practical suggestions to help
young families cope.

Matthew Ies Spetter, PhD
Family and Marriage Counselor
Founder of the Riverdale Mental Health Clinic
Author and teacher

Ms. Griffin's recommendations for parenting are
based on her expert knowledge and her dedication
to each child's needs. Each time we have sought Ms.
Griffin's advice (regarding eating, sleeping, and toilet
training issues), she has provided my husband and
me with suggestions that have yielded 100 percent
success. Being a parent is my greatest joy, and Ms.
Griffin has given our family the common sense tools
that enable us to show unconditional love to our two
girls while we parent responsibly.

Janine and Jay McLear
parents of a two- and four-year-old

I found this book to be a wonderful resource when looking for help in dealing with childhood behavioral problems. The author writes with sensitivity and offers solutions that promise to help develop self-discipline in your child. The book is written in a clear and easy-to-understand style.

Joan Coplan, MS
early childhood education

This book reflects Ms. Griffin's sensitivity and understanding of children and is certain to ease the apprehension parents feel about various home and school issues. Ms.Griffin offers excellent practical advice. *My Child Won't Listen: ...and other early childhood problems* is a must-read for parents and teachers.

Bernice Schatz
former elementary school principal

MY CHILD WON'T LISTEN...

and other early childhood problems

Linda Griffin, MS

authorHOUSE®

AuthorHouse™
1663 Liberty Drive, Suite 200
Bloomington, IN 47403
www.authorhouse.com
Phone: 1-800-839-8640

First published by AuthorHouse 3/13/2009

ISBN: 978-1-4389-1690-3 (sc)

Library of Congress Control Number: 2009900765

Printed in the United States of America
Bloomington, Indiana

This book is printed on acid-free paper.

This book is dedicated, with much love and admiration, to my mom.

ACKNOWLEDGMENTS

I want to thank Lisa Gibson for editing the original magazine articles. Also, many years ago, she taught me how to use my first word processing program, and for that I will always be grateful.

***

Thanks to Amy, David, Richard, Susan, and Iliana for being such a wonderful and supportive family.

TABLE OF CONTENTS

INTRODUCTION

What makes this different from other books about parenting is the experience I bring to writing it. Teaching young children for more than thirty years has allowed me to connect with the lives of many families. Every November and March, when I complete another round of parent-teacher conferences, I think about the impact of parent-child relationships and the significance of my role as teacher in the social and emotional development of the children in my care. Through the years, I have been privileged to have parents confide in me and seek my counsel as a teacher, parent, and stepparent.

Many years ago, I worked with Faye Gerace, a friend and esteemed early childhood educator in The Early Language Program. Under the direction of Dr. Seymour Perlin, who conceived the program, Faye and I worked with parents and their three-and-a-half-year-old children in a learning project together. Here, parents, together with younger siblings, stayed to observe and play with their children in a nursery school setting. What transpired was immediately discussed in the ongoing parent discussion group. This unique setting gave me the opportunity to observe firsthand the interaction of parent and child and to foster positive changes through modeling behavior. I've always believed parenting is a skill that can be learned, and the result of this three-year, federally funded project has proved that to be true.

In the years that followed, I matched parenting styles with the behavioral problems I saw in my first-grade and kindergarten classrooms. Teaching provided the ideal setting for observing many different child behaviors. I saw how children interacted with their peers and other adults, how they handled routines or the lack of them, and how some children enjoyed challenges while others were easily frustrated. I saw children who tested adult authority every chance they had and others who behaved well even when provoked. I saw children who took care of their belongings and worked independently, while others needed constant adult supervision. Every day, I watched and supported children as they worked and played. As a teacher, parent, and stepparent, I had to deal with many of the problems I discuss in this book.

In addition, parent–teacher conferences taught me why and how parents disciplined their children. Insights about child behavior developed as patterns emerged. The more I spoke with parents, the more I realized the enormous influence parents have on their children. As you read this book, these patterns will become clear. They will give you insight into why problems arise, as well as the skills to fix them.

After obtaining my master's degree in counseling, I advised parents privately and conducted parenting workshops. *My Child Won't Listen . . . and other early childhood problems* is a compilation of articles I wrote for *Suburban Parenting News*. Some articles have been reworked, and others have been added. I wanted to put together a book that would help parents live with kids and like it. Too often, I've heard the frustration and seen the tears of parents trying to cope. "I thought," said a distraught mother of two boys, age five and three, "that being a mom would be fun. It hasn't been fun yet." Another mother confessed, "I haven't said this to anyone, but there are times when I think it would have been better not to have had children." Obviously, something has gone wrong to make parents feel this way.

I have come to the conclusion that most parent-child problems are caused by parents not knowing what behavior is reasonable at a particular age. Problems occur when parental expectations are too great, too small, unclear, or inconsistent. When expectations are too great, children can be made to feel inadequate. The message they get is that whatever they do is not good enough. This can cause some children to feel resentful or hostile. Since they can never please their parents, they give up trying. On the other hand, parents who expect too little from their child may raise a child who is dependent and insecure. The child may exhibit infantile behavior or become easily frustrated. Finally, unclear or inconsistent expectations are confusing to children and can result in manipulative behavior. You will learn how to prevent these troubling behaviors from taking hold and will also find out how to fix them.

I've also written this book for educators and other professionals who work with young children. The strategies that are offered in this book apply in the classroom or at home. Also, educational issues are dealt with from both the parents' and teachers' points of view. Most importantly, I discuss how to help young children handle conflict. Recently, a young teacher witnessed two first-graders hitting each other. She looked at me, bewildered, and said, "What should I do with them?" I answer that question for parents and professionals. Discipline is the single most important issue a teacher must deal with. Without control of the class, even a well-prepared lesson has little value.

All through the book, you will learn how to set limits in a fair and firm way and find out why I don't believe in giving children second chances once rules have been established.

My Child Won't Listen . . . and other early childhood problems is an upbeat, practical, no-nonsense book filled with real-life examples of child behavior. I selected vignettes that are representative of the most common problems that I have experienced through the years. The stories are all true, but people's names and other identifying characteristics have been changed.

MY CHILD
WON'T LISTEN . . .

**and other early childhood
problems**

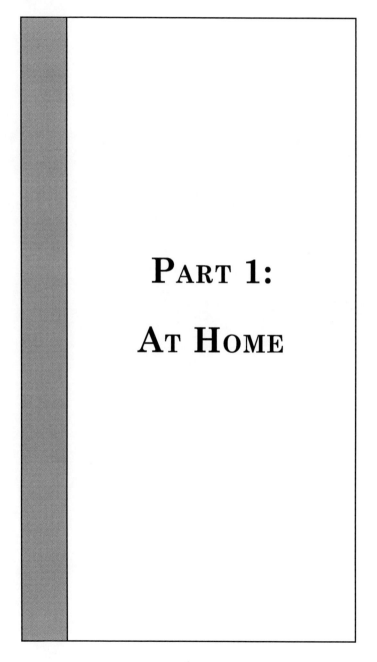

PART 1:

AT HOME

WHY TIME-OUT DOESN'T WORK

Most parents tell me that time-out doesn't work. I always respond with "allowing a child to cool off for a few minutes in a quiet place can help calm things, but, by itself, it does not change behavior." Usually, parents are relieved to know that other moms and dads have experienced the same poor result from time-out.

Time-out is used by parents as a way to discipline a child who is fighting with a sibling, having a temper tantrum, interrupting an adult discussion, being unruly at the dinner table, or refusing to listen. In many families, time-out is used almost exclusively as a way to discipline a disruptive child—and herein lies the problem.

In order for discipline to be effective, it must teach a child what is acceptable behavior, take into account a child's age and emotional maturity, and whenever possible be directly related to the child's objectionable behavior. In addition, for change to take place, parents must be committed and consistent and must make their child's behavior a top priority. Following are some examples of discipline which relate to the factors mentioned above:

> When two-and-a-half-year-old Sam drew on a living room wall, Mom and Dad gave him time-out. It was not long before Sam was drawing on the wall again. His parents found it more effective to say *no* and immediately give Sam paper to draw on while saying firmly, "You draw on paper, not walls." When Sam's parents repeated this several times, Sam eventually got the message to draw on paper. Sam wanted his parents' approval, so he complied with their wishes.

If Sam were a year or two older, the approach to his drawing on walls should be different; the goal should then be to help him control his impulses and develop a conscience. The verbal response to Sam's behavior needs to be the same, but he should not be permitted to draw at that time. Instead, he must be given a sponge and cleanser and asked to wash off the crayon marks. This reinforces the idea that he was responsible for the mess. A short time-out should follow. In a period of calm, his parents ought to express their displeasure and set consequences if the incident is ever repeated. Children need to feel their parents' disapproval. Not everything a child does is okay.

> When six-year-old Susan hurt her younger brother, she was given time-out. Although this was an appropriate course of action, at the time it was not enough to stop Susan from continuing to hurt her brother. Her negative feelings about her brother, whose behavior had been intrusive, needed to be validated; her belongings needed to be protected from him; and she needed more positive attention. But along with more physical and verbal expressions of love, her parents also needed to set and discuss consequences before she acted aggressively again.

What is the difference between a punishment and a consequence?

Punishment is typically dispensed immediately after misbehavior. The child may be out of control, and the parent may act out of anger. The parent may often make threats that he or she is unwilling or unable to carry out. A consequence is set in a period of calm. The parent is in control and spells out a loss of a privilege that is age-appropriate and that will be carried out. It then becomes the *child's choice* to behave appropriately or not.

> When five-year-old Billy had a temper tantrum in the family room, his parents put him in his bedroom for time-out. Billy kept running back into the family room, screaming at the top of his lungs. Each time his parents put him back in his room, he came out again. Often, Billy's parents gave in to his demands because they could not deal with his behavior. Billy continued to have tantrums.

In order to change Billy's behavior, his parents had to make a pledge not to give in to his tantrums. *Billy had tantrums because they worked.* The new expectation, that Billy would not have tantrums, was discussed. Billy was told that if he misbehaved in that way again, he would be ignored. Instead of dragging Billy to his room for time-out, Mom and Dad walked away from Billy when he was out of control. When Mom and Dad changed their response to Billy's tantrums, his behavior started to improve.

> Samantha was refusing to turn off the computer when her mother said dinner was ready. This always escalated into a screaming match. Samantha would be out of control, and Mother would send her to her room for time-out.

Here again, Samantha's behavior didn't change until her mother did things differently. First, Mother made her expectations clear, promising to give Samantha a five-minute warning before dinnertime. Samantha was told that if she didn't comply, she would not be allowed to use the computer for a full day. In order for Mother to remain in control of the situation, *it was important that she follow through* with the consequence in a calm, matter-of-fact manner and not respond to Samantha's bargaining. When Samantha's mother was firm and consistent, Samantha started to listen.

I often see parents who are locked into unproductive patterns of behavior and need help to do things differently. Often, they've used time-out because, even though it didn't work, at least they felt they were doing *something*. Many parents who come to me for advice tell me they have tried everything to change their child's behavior, but nothing has worked. But while they have often tried many things, they haven't spent enough time on any one method. So, after reading this book and digesting the suggestions, make a plan and stick to it. It usually takes about two weeks to see some improvement. Also, it is helpful to think of ways to short-circuit unwanted behavior before it escalates. In conclusion, be selective about your use of time-out, and be aware of its limitations.

Bonding versus Crazy Glue: What's the Difference?

Bonding is essential for healthy child development. It is a special closeness between parent and child that takes into account the child's need to separate from the parent and develop a sense of autonomy. Bonding as if with crazy glue keeps a child dependent. Parents who apply heavy doses of crazy glue always seem to have a reason why they must continue to foster dependence in their children. As you read the statements below, ask yourself the following question: Does the statement reflect the need of the parent or that of the child?

> "I wipe his bottom because he doesn't do a good job." (parent of a five-year-old)

"She won't go to sleep unless she is in our bed." (parent of a two-year-old)

"Take the diaper off him and put on training pants? You've got to be kidding!" (parent of a child who was almost three years old but not yet toilet-trained)

"She won't get enough milk if I don't give her the bottle." (parent of a three-year-old)

"He won't eat his pancakes unless I cut them up for him." (parent of a seven-year-old)

This kind of parenting often produces children who have trouble adjusting to school and become increasingly difficult at home. They may exhibit immature behavior because they have been infantilized. Their behavior may be manipulative because they have their parents doing their bidding, or fearful because they have been made to feel they cannot survive without their parents.

How do you know if you are applying crazy glue? Ask yourself the following questions:

1. Is my child's behavior immature compared with that of his peers?

2. Does my child have difficulty functioning without me?

3. Does my child demand my attention most of the time?

4. Is my child's behavior interfering with other family relationships?

5. Do other significant people say that my child is spoiled?

6. Is my child reluctant to try new things at home or in school?

7. *Whose needs are being met by what I am doing—mine or those of my child?*

Parents who find it difficult to get "unglued" can profit from joining a parenting group or from seeking counseling.

Setting Limits

"My child won't listen."

"The grandparents say our children are out of control."

"My spouse says I spoil our daughter."

Are you pleading, threatening, scolding, bribing, hitting, yelling, and not getting any results? The following are incidents parents discussed with me in the course of our parenting sessions. I have selected the most common parental reactions to misbehavior and have offered more productive alternative ways to respond.

Driving with Jennifer

Mr. J. explained what happened when he took his six-year-old for a drive:

Jennifer refused to put on her seat belt. I told her I couldn't drive the car unless her seat belt was fastened. Jennifer yelled that she didn't want to put it on. I told her she could get hurt if I stopped short, but Jennifer became more obstinate. I tried to reason with her. I told her it's against the law to drive without seat belts fastened. When that didn't work, I told her that if the car crashed, her head would hit the windshield. In desperation, I added that she could wind up in the hospital. Finally, I lost my temper, screamed that she had ruined my day, and forcibly put the seat belt on a hysterical child.

In the course of our sessions, it became clear that Mr. J. believed that if he presented reasonable arguments, he would get Jennifer to do what he wanted. Like so many bright, articulate parents, Mr. J. often "explained" too much, and Jennifer tuned out.

I suggested that Mr. J. discuss his expectations beforehand and let Jennifer know what the consequences would be if they were not met. Jennifer needed to be told that she must not make a fuss when putting on her seat belt or she would not be allowed to go for the ride. It was important that Mr. J. be prepared to leave Jennifer with another adult or to abandon his plans if necessary. Setting limits works only if parents give it top priority. I suggested that, even if Jennifer decided to put her seat belt on after making a fuss, the expectations should be calmly repeated, and the drive cancelled. This puts Dad in control and discourages manipulative behavior in the future.

Banking with Christopher

Mrs. C. went to the bank with four-year-old Christopher, and this is what happened:

> I was filling out my deposit slip when Christopher climbed onto the counter and began pulling out deposit, withdrawal, and checking slips from their slots. I yelled at him to stop. When Christopher continued to misbehave, I told him that the bank manager was going to throw him out of the bank. Christopher didn't seem to care.

Mrs. C. often used threats in an attempt to get Christopher to behave. The threats didn't work, and Christopher was out of control. It became clear in our discussions that Mrs. C. often made threats that could not be carried out. Additionally, I helped Mrs. C. understand that the purpose of discipline is to teach children what is acceptable behavior. It was important that Christopher learn to respect property—not because the bank manager might throw him out but because his mother expected him to behave in a particular way. Only then could Mrs. C. impart her values to Christopher and help him develop inner control.

Shopping with Isabel

Mrs. I. described what happened when she went shopping with her three-year-old daughter, Isabel:

> I was standing at the checkout counter when Isabel began pushing our shopping cart into the woman standing in front of us. I told Isabel to stop it, but she ignored me. I repeated myself many times and each time got louder. Isabel stopped only after the woman looked at me in disgust and angrily reprimanded Isabel.

Mrs. I. failed to do the most important thing—to take Isabel by the hand and keep her away from the shopping cart. Mrs. I. confessed in our parenting sessions that she often made reprimands or requests but never followed through with an action. Isabel had learned not to take her mother seriously.

How to Set Limits

1. Whenever possible, it is best to discuss your expectations beforehand.

2. Move close to your child when you ask him/her to do something.

3. Praise your child before he/she has a chance to misbehave.

4. Make the consequences of misbehavior clear, and always follow through.

5. Keep explanations short and to the point.

6. Do not give second chances. It encourages children to be manipulative.

7. If your child misbehaves in a public place, be prepared to leave if the need arises. You

will succeed in setting limits only if your child's behavior becomes your top priority.

8. Be consistent!

In addition, help your child become a better listener by not repeating yourself after you give directions. Make sure your child knows you will say things just one time. I know what you're thinking—*that will never work!* The goal is for improvement, and if you use praise and rewards in conjunction with being consistent, then your child will become a better listener.

Bedtime Is a Nightmare, and Mealtime Can be Madness

Bedtime Is a Nightmare

Is your child refusing to sleep in his/her own bed? Is it causing conflict in your marriage? This problem is easily avoided but difficult to correct. I found that children who sleep in bed with their parents are usually children who rule the roost and consistently give their parents a difficult time. They buck their parents whenever possible and are constantly testing house rules. Their parents are exhausted, first from getting a poor night's sleep, and second from dealing with a demanding child.

Children need boundaries. They need to respect their parents' right to be a couple. Also, the ability to fall asleep alone is a skill children need to learn on the road to becoming autonomous. After helping many parents deal with this issue, I have discovered that when parents succeeded in helping children sleep in their own beds, other behavioral problems also dramatically improved. I believe this happens because parents regain control.

Avoid the problem by always comforting your child in his/her own bed. It's all too easy to fall into the trap of taking a crying child to bed with you. Parents defend their actions by saying they are exhausted and need to get some sleep. Unfortunately, this is very shortsighted. Once a child has established a pattern of sleeping in your bed, be prepared for many sleepless and sexless nights before the problem is corrected. To change course, talk to your child in an age-appropriate way, and explain the new rules: "From now on, you will be sleeping in your own bed." Then, follow the suggestions in the next paragraph. Be prepared for things to get worse before they get better. Remember, it is extremely important to be consistent. Any backsliding on your part will compound the problem and make it more difficult to change the behavior.

Is your child staying up later and later? Does he/she want another glass of water, another story read, and just one more kiss? Children need and want routines; it makes them feel secure. Work out a schedule with your child, and put it in chart form, using pictures from magazines. The chart might show a child brushing his teeth; another might show a child listening to a story, etc. Some five-year-olds and older children can put a check mark next to each routine as it is completed. Younger children can point to what comes next. Adapt the idea, so your child participates as much as his/her ability allows. It is important not to deviate from the established routine. If you stick to it, you will begin to see improvement over time. So hang in there!

Mealtime Can Be Madness

Mealtime at the Smith family gave everyone indigestion. Mrs. Smith begged, bribed, and prodded three-year-old Meghan to eat. Food was the topic of discussion, and Meghan was repeatedly asked to take one more bite. At the Jones family, Billy jumped up and down in the dining room chair, demanding to play or watch

TV. Often, his parents gave in and allowed him to eat while he watched television in the den.

Does any of this sound familiar? If so, remember that even the youngest child can be expected to sit at the table until he finishes his meal. The trick is to make portions small enough to enable your child to easily clean his plate. Often, children feel overwhelmed by large portions of food. It is helpful to serve *very* small portions on a salad plate, so children have the opportunity to ask for more if they choose. This simple suggestion can turn mealtime around by allowing your child to meet with success and by giving you the opportunity to praise your child for a job well done. Also, take advantage of dinnertime to talk about your day, not about food.

Share experiences; listen to each other. Use mealtime to become closer as a family. Relax; it is common for children to eat poorly at one meal but make up for it at another. Make sure to discuss your new mealtime expectations beforehand, and approach meals in a positive, optimistic way. (Go to *A Myth: The "Children Know Best" Philosophy"* for help with picky eaters.)

What Children Can't Tell You

Seven-year-old Marc was angry. He had recently thrown ice at a child in the school yard and had kicked another child in the groin. According to Marc's teacher and parents, he had been a bright, verbal, and well-behaved first-grader until a month or so ago. Marc's parents were horrified by his aggressive behavior, but didn't know what to do about it.

When Marc's parents came to see me, they were carrying their sixteen-month-old daughter, Beth. During our initial interview, I was struck by the warm, caring feelings the parents had for each other and their children. I asked the parents if they could think of any change that might account for Marc's acting out. "No," they replied. Routines were the same. There was no unusual job, marital, or health-related stress to report. I looked up at angelic Beth and said, "I bet Beth is at an age now where she gets into Marc's things."

"Does she ever!" was the reply. With a little prodding, the parents quickly realized why Marc was so angry. Beth frequently messed up Marc's toys, and on one occasion she had knocked down all his books. To make matters worse, Marc's parents made him clean up. "Boy, was Marc angry," his father said.

"For good reason," I added.

"Beth's behavior has certainly upset Marc, but we never put it together with his problems at school," exclaimed Marc's mother.

Marc couldn't tell his parents how important it was for his belongings to be protected from his sister. He couldn't say that he felt resentful and angry because he was expected to share all his toys. Instead Marc did the only thing he could do—act out.

Five-year old Liz was clingy. She constantly followed her mother around the house and had great difficulty playing alone. At school, she was unable to focus and required a great deal of individual attention. Liz's parents didn't know what to make of her demanding behavior. They tried spending more time with her, and they also tried ignoring her demands for constant company. They came to see me when they didn't know what else to do.

What Liz couldn't tell her parents was that she felt frightened. She heard her parents argue. She heard her mother threaten to leave. Liz couldn't say that her worst fear was that of being abandoned. She couldn't say how this preoccupied her thoughts and made it difficult for her to function in school.

John was easily frustrated. He cried when things didn't go his way. He cried when children mildly criticized something he did or said. He wailed when children called him a crybaby. According to John's parents, he had little difficulty at home, but they were concerned about his sensitivity and wanted to know how to toughen him up.

John couldn't say that, as an only child, he dealt mainly with reasonable adults who always treated him fairly. John couldn't say that he didn't have the experience of dealing with a sibling who pushed, shoved, or teased him. Therefore, he often overreacted to his peers' behavior. John wasn't able to tell his parents that it was important for him to have more playmates and sleepovers.

Eight-year-old Nancy stopped completing her schoolwork. Workbook pages were incomplete, and homework wasn't getting done. Nancy's parents tried taking away privileges—no more television or video games. They tried giving her extra schoolwork to do at home as punishment. They tried talking to Nancy, but she couldn't articulate why her work wasn't getting done.

Nancy couldn't say that since her dog died, she had been grieving and unable to concentrate. Nancy couldn't say that she needed to talk and draw pictures about her beloved four-footed friend. (Her parents believed talking about it upset Nancy more.)

Susan complained of aches and pains every day she attended kindergarten. One time, she touched a freckle on her hand and tearfully proclaimed that she had the chicken pox. She wanted to go home.

Susan was a bright, articulate child who enjoyed class activities. She would become upset during transition times. While the teacher tried to comfort Susan, Susan spoke freely about missing her mother who had worked since she was a few months old: "Mommy goes shopping on Saturday, and I go to school on Sunday. I don't see her very much."

Mr. and Mrs. S. stated that they didn't understand why Susan was having such a problem. After all, Mrs. S. had gone back to work when Susan was just a few months old. They said, "Susan should be used to being away from us." What Susan couldn't say is that for her to become independent, she must first be dependent. Secure children can separate from their parents; insecure children cannot.

Susan's parents had been handling the problem by telling her she was acting like a baby, and they showed their annoyance by withdrawing from her—all of which exacerbated the problem. Susan couldn't tell her parents that what she needed was *more* attention and *more* affection. Only then would she be able to separate from them successfully.

There are times when parents need to play detective. Often, the cause of behavior is not readily apparent. During parenting sessions, I often ask the following questions to help parents zero in on the cause of a problem behavior:

1. When did the problem behavior start?

2. What was life like in the family during that time?

3. Have any significant changes taken place in the family?

4. Has any family member been under an unusual amount of stress?

5. What is the child's perception of the parents' relationship to each other and to siblings?

Remember that young children want very much to please their parents and teachers. They want to be good. When something gets in the way of good behavior, it is imperative that parents search out the cause, since, more often than not, children can't tell you what is bothering them.

FRENETIC FOURS

I am struck by the fact that the majority of parents who are in need of parenting advice have four-year-old children. After a brief reprieve from the terrible twos, parents find themselves dealing with the excessive behavior of a four-year-old. This prompted me to find a word that encapsulated four-year-old behavior and, not to be outdone by the "terrible twos," also begins with the "f" sound. My list included foolish, frantic, funny, and phooey. Although four-year-olds can be all these things, I settled on frenetic.

Four-year-olds bring to mind German shepherd puppies. Their paws are too big for their bodies, and they seem to trip over themselves. Walk into a classroom of four-year-olds, and you are almost certain to see a child falling off a chair. And, just like a puppy, a four-year-old defies you. He tests you to the limit. The first thing parents of four-year-olds tell me is "my child won't listen." Sound familiar? These parents have described whining, regressive and obstinate behavior, and acting out. In addition, much to the concern of parents, four-year-olds enjoy using bathroom words. Also, they may respond to stress by having "accidents" or tummy aches. It seems that nothing a four-year-old does is in moderation. Parents are justifiably exhausted.

The Last Bounce Theory

Billy was playing ball outside when his mother called him in for dinner. Although she alerted Billy five minutes ahead of time that dinner would be served shortly, Billy continued to bounce the ball after the final call for dinner was announced. Mother started shouting, and Billy got more belligerent. By the time this incident was over, Billy was crying, and Mother had lost control. Neither of them had much of an appetite. My suggestion to the parents was to short-circuit this scenario by not responding to the extra bounce. Expect it, ignore it, and do not get angry. A simple "let's go inside" while walking away is usually sufficient. If that doesn't work, dispassionately take the ball away and walk inside the house. The objective is to eliminate escalation of the incident while remaining in control.

The "No More Junk Food" Plan

Katie always caused a scene in the supermarket. She wanted more candy or a sugarcoated cereal with little nutritional value. Rather than deal with an out-of-control child, Mother usually gave in to Katie's demands. Katie became more and more difficult. Our plan to make shopping more pleasant was as follows:

1. Mother would clearly state her expectations before she entered the supermarket.

2. Mother would remind Katie that after the first time she misbehaved, they would immediately leave the store.

3. Mother would encourage Katie to participate in the shopping expedition by giving her jobs to do. For example, Katie might be asked to put fruit in a plastic bag, count potatoes, or locate and point to items that are on the shopping list as they walk through the store together.

4. Mother would carry out the plan calmly. (This is key to the plan's success.)

5. Mother would praise Katie often when her behavior was appropriate.

Mother's initial response to this plan was negative. The thought of leaving a cart full of food in the store while carrying a screaming child outside did not appeal to her. She felt she was the one being punished. I assured her it would not happen more than a few times before Katie got the message. Katie's behavior would improve only when Katie saw that her mother was serious and willing to take action.

Mother followed the supermarket plan and reported that it took only one episode to change Katie's behavior!

Help for Living with a Four-Year-Old

Many parents are comforted by knowing what to expect at various ages and stages. Learning what typical behavior is for a given age allows parents to plan strategies for coping. *Remember that just because it is "a stage" does not mean you should ignore objectionable behavior.*

Remember also that children mature at different rates. Not all four-year-olds are at the same stage of emotional, physical, or social development.

1. When dealing with a four-year-old, think about the point where things deteriorate, and work out a plan to intercept it.

2. Set priorities. Allow your child to assert himself/herself by having the last bounce. (Safety issues are exempt from this theory.)

3. Always discuss your expectations and the consequences for inappropriate behavior beforehand.

4. Praise good behavior.

5. Be consistent.

A Myth: "The Children Know Best" Philosophy

Most people agree it is best to feed an infant on demand. Rigid schedules are a thing of the past. Even so, there are times when parents must gently help a baby extend the time between feedings or help the baby differentiate between day and night. Some parents, however, take the position that children have an innate ability to know what is right and defer to them on a variety of issues. Following are some examples of the "children know best" philosophy, carried to an extreme.

Shari was a little girl in my kindergarten class who became sick in school and went home with a high fever. I was surprised when I saw Shari and her mother appear at the classroom door early the next morning. When I inquired about how Shari was feeling, Mother replied: "Oh, she still has fever, but she wanted to go to school. I gave her two aspirin." I strongly suggested that Mother take Shari home and let her rest in bed—that it was not in Shari's best interest or fair to the other children for Shari to be in school. "But she doesn't want to go home," said Mother.

"You're the adult," I replied. "It is not a child's decision."

Tommy had difficulty separating from his mother when school began in September. We worked out a plan where Mother would gradually spend less time in the classroom each day. After a while, I determined that Tommy was able to function without his mother present. When Tommy cried, Mother was instructed to say, "You really are able to stay without me. I'll see you later." Then we planned for her to make a quick exit. Tommy's crying stopped shortly after his mother left, and he enjoyed the activities. Tommy had a very productive year.

The following year, Tommy again had difficulty separating from his mother as he began first grade. This time, his teacher and the school guidance counselor decided that Mother should stay in school until Tommy told her to leave. He never did. Mother sat outside the classroom door the entire school year, and Tommy regressed emotionally. The guidance counselor believed that Tommy knew best, and Mother, because of her own insecurities, didn't have the strength to take a stand on her own. It is not uncommon for children to be clingy at the beginning of the school year. The adults in this situation abrogated their responsibility to help Tommy overcome his fear.

Here is another example of a child being allowed to make adult decisions. Rose was in my first-grade class many years ago. Mother firmly believed that Rose should not be required to do anything she did not want to do. That included her homework, completing work in school, or going on class trips. "Rose," I was told, "should not have to conform." Rose was a very unhappy child who frequently had temper tantrums, had no friends in class, and who, unfortunately, grew up to be a very unhappy adult. Mother didn't realize that Rose was frightened by having control over things she didn't understand or have the experience to deal with.

...s three-and-a-half years old when ...ts came to see me for advice. Her ...as concerned that Jenna was very immature for her age. Jenna would curl up in a fetal position, would often use baby talk, and inappropriately tug on her parents' hair or clothing. In my presence, Jenna pulled on her mother's blouse, screaming, "I want a snack," at which time her mother breast-fed her. Jenna's parents believed that Jenna would give up the breast on her own. They chose not to connect Jenna's immature behavior with the fact that she was being treated like an infant. *Children need help and encouragement to move on to the next stage of emotional development, and sometimes that means gratification must be delayed or denied.*

Similarly, I have had parents come to me for help because their children were still in diapers at age four. One parent told me she didn't want to do anything that would upset her daughter. Another parent asked me for a gentle way of fixing the problem. In every case, the children were experiencing social problems which, in turn, were causing behavioral problems. Parents got into this predicament because they believed their children would become toilet trained when they were ready, with little if any parental intervention. In some cases, that works. However, for most families, parents must make their expectations known and take action; otherwise, they risk having their children stuck and unable to move on to the next stage of development.

Susan's mother called me after returning from a stressful week—a long visit to Grandma's house. At home, the "children know best" philosophy had been followed, and Susan was allowed to dictate the menu. At her grandparent's house, Susan always wanted food that was not being served, and her grandmother refused to give it to her. Susan's father complained to me that she was a very picky eater and had caused a scene at every meal.

My view is that parents have the responsibility to serve healthy, tasty meals. The child may choose how much he/she eats of what is served. If these principles had been established early on, then Mom and Dad would not find it necessary to be short-order cooks. Establishing such principles at home can help children in social situations outside of the home (there are many times when the choice of what to eat is not an option). Children also learn to respect the time and effort that goes into preparing a meal. Children need adults to nurture, love, and provide them with support as they tackle the tasks of growing up. Judith Viorst in her book *Necessary Losses* put it succinctly: "Everybody needs some frustration to grow on."

HELPING YOUR CHILD DEAL WITH AGGRESSIVE CHILDREN

A day doesn't go by when a child isn't pushed, hit, or teased in school. It frequently happens in the school yard, lunchroom, or on the school bus—places where the ratio of adults to children is minimal, and supervision is difficult. But even at home, a playdate can quickly turn into a battle over a toy or not wanting to play a particular game.

Some children are instructed by their parents to strike back, others to walk away and tell the nearest adult. But the goal, in my opinion, should be to use conflict as a way of teaching children how to talk to each other and, ultimately, to become responsible for resolving problems on their own.

For instance, a typical scenario between six-year-olds goes like this:

Billy: John hit me!

Mother: John, don't hit Billy. It's not nice.

John: But he hit me first!

Mother: Why don't you both say you're sorry and go play?

In this case, Mother takes on the primary role of ending the conflict. Her immediate (understandable) objective is peace, which she may achieve temporarily. However, in the long run, the children are not learning how to resolve their differences.

This chapter will help parents give their young school-age children the necessary skills to handle such incidents in a way that lets them feel less victimized and more in control—a tall order for young children, maybe, but it can be accomplished with practice and adult guidance. The following are actual dialogues between first-grade boys. I asked the victim to tell his attacker what he was angry about; often, this meant redirecting the children to speak to each other rather than to me.

Incident One

> **Billy:** You started to fight me over there. You spoiled my day.

Steven: You said you wanted to fight me yesterday.

> **Billy:** But I lied about that. You should know that.

Steven: How should I know that?

Incident Two

> **Bob:** You were hitting me!

> **Evan:** You hitted me!

> **Bob:** First you were in back, and then you skipped me [referring to standing in line].

> **Evan:** You were the one who was hitting me all over.

Incident Three

Ira: You scratched me right here.

James: You scratched me. When I was going down the stairs, you pushed me down on the floor and scratched me here! Don't do it again.

Ira: Sorry, James.

The first two examples show how important it is for adults not to take on the role of judge and jury. There is no way you can know what really happened. The children in the third incident have had training and practice with verbal exchanges of this kind. From this position of strength, James elicits an apology and walks away feeling vindicated.

In order to help children get out their anger, I encourage them to say any of the following:

That hurt!

Don't do it again!

It made me angry when you hit me! Stop it!

Keep in mind that children resolve things in unique ways. On one occasion, two little girls complained to me about each other and began to yell the following:

> You bothered me!

> No, I didn't!

> Yes, you did!

> No, I didn't!

> Yes, you did!

This went on for several minutes until they both started laughing and walked away. During this interchange, I stood quietly by and allowed them to work out their problem. It is important not to impose adult standards on what constitutes conflict resolution for young children. Both children were satisfied with the outcome and played happily with each other after they left me.

Remember

1. Have children talk to each other—not to you. You may need to supply the words until your child gets the hang of it. Say: "Tell

Mary she hurt you and that she should not do it again."

2. Encourage your children to make eye contact with any child who allegedly hurts them. Say: "Look at John when you say that."

3. Resist taking on the role of judge and jury. In most cases, you will never know what really happened unless you were there to witness the incident.

4. Suggest that your child use a loud voice. In order to make an impact, louder is better. Help your child practice.

5. In fact, the best way to have children become comfortable with these suggestions is to practice them at home. Role-play verbal exchanges with your child.

Helping a Child Cope with Death

What Death Means to a Child

When my brother was four years old, our parakeet died. Richy walked over to the cage and exclaimed, "Who shot 'im?" After examining the dead bird, he turned to me, his twelve-year-old sister, and asked, "When will he get up and fly?"

"The bird is dead," I responded. "It will never fly again."

Richy's response was typical of a four-year-old. For that age, death is reversible, and little emotion is connected with it. Five-year-olds may see death as an "end" but can only understand it in concrete terms of what a pet can no longer do. Although six-year-olds have a slightly better understanding that old people will die, they, too, can still believe that death is reversible. It is not until age seven that many children have a reasonable concept of death. They are scared of it, yet they are fascinated by it.

Children experience death by the reactions of the people around them. They experience it when a beloved member of the family is missing. When one of my first-graders, Bobby, lost his grandma, the children made the following comments:

"My cat died because he was sick."

"My dog died because he had a heart attack."

I then asked, "How did you know your pet was dead?"

"If you can't listen to their heart."

"When they are not breathing."

"It's not running around."

"If their eyes are not open."

"They are bleeding."

"They're cold."

"My rabbit was stiff. He was like a rock."

After hearing the others, Bobby felt comfortable enough to talk about his grandma. "They had to bury her. When they die, they see God. I feel sad. I used to read a book with her. I used to color with her. She loved coloring."

Another child spoke up: "My poppy died. His heart wasn't beating fast enough. He goes up to heaven because God takes his soul. You bury them. I forget the rest.... When people die, someone comes next to them and says something about them, and when they're finished, we go home."

How Parents Can Help Young Children Cope

It is best to assess what a child's concept of death is before launching into any explanation. A simple "what do you think happens when someone dies?" will allow you to clarify any misconceptions based on your child's emotional and intellectual development. Answer questions simply and directly. Do not over-explain.

Although our religious beliefs sometimes determine our concepts of death and dying, there are some things we can do, no matter what our orientation:

1. It is important not to frighten children by equating death with sleep. They are not the same. Say "the dog has died" rather than "we put the dog to sleep."

2. Assure your child that there is always someone to love and take care of children. A young child's worst fear is that of being abandoned.

3. Include children in the mourning process. Use your judgment in excluding young children from parts of a funeral that might be unnecessarily frightening. It is helpful to assign a supportive, caring adult to attend to your child during services.

4. Share stories about the deceased. Encourage your child to draw pictures of things they did together.

5. Express your sorrow in words your child can understand: "Mommy is crying because she will miss Grandma very much."

6. It is generally better to tell your child the truth about an impending death. A child's imagination can be far more grotesque than reality.

7. Children should be allowed to mourn for a dead pet. They can bury the pet with adult help and write or draw on a rock to make a headstone. Pictures of the pet can be displayed at home and talked about. Do not suggest replacing a pet right away.

8. Read age-appropriate books about the subject of death to your child. The following list, courtesy of the Ossining Public Library, might be helpful:

   About Dying by Sara Stein

   How It Feels When a Parent Dies by Jill Krementz

   I Had a Friend Named Peter by Janice Cohn

   Let's Talk about Death and Dying by Bruce Sanders

   The Kids' Book about Death and Dying by Eric Rofes

The Saddest Time by Norma Simon

When a Pet Dies by Fred Rogers

"My Child Didn't Do It"

As parents, we have a responsibility to protect our children. Sometimes it's difficult to know when to step in and when to hold back. The following true story illustrates what happens when parents deny their children's behavior problems and shield them from experiencing the consequences of their negative behavior.

In kindergarten, Joey hit, kicked, and pushed other children. He didn't follow any rules. He didn't have to—his mother and father always defended his right to misbehave. Mr. and Mrs. J. blamed the other children for provoking Joey. They said the teacher picked on their son or that the school aides didn't watch him properly in the lunchroom or yard. Mr. and Mrs. J. vented their anger at the principal, at the teacher, or at anyone who would listen to their complaints.

By third grade, the few friends that Joey had were the school troublemakers. He was in constant fights. When Joey didn't do his homework, his parents sent notes to the teacher asking her to excuse him: "Joey had to go to sleep early." "Relatives were visiting." "He didn't understand the assignment." "The dog ate it." There were a few times when Joey's parents did his homework for him. They didn't want Joey to get "bad marks." Mrs. J. blamed the other children for being a bad influence on Joey. "Joey," she said, "was being bullied." When the teacher refused to take Joey on a school trip because he had hurt a classmate, Mrs. J. went directly to the principal and insisted that Joey be allowed to go along.

In junior high school, Joey had a reputation for being disruptive in class, and his outbursts became more frequent. Joey believed it was everybody else's fault; he never understood his role in the events that happened. On one occasion, Joey came home from school in tears and told his mother that a bunch of boys had jumped him in gym and banged his head against a metal locker. Mrs. J., in her usual fashion, went to the school, demanding punishment for the offenders and protection for her son.

She found out that Joey had prevented the class from going outdoors by not getting into his gym clothes in a timely fashion. The kids asked Joey to get ready and sit down in front of the locker, so they could go out to play. Joey said they couldn't tell him what to do because they weren't his teacher. At that point, a group of boys forcibly pushed Joey down against his locker.

By the time Mrs. J. sought help for Joey, he was a freshman in high school and had gotten arrested for disorderly conduct while under the influence of alcohol. Mrs. J. sought help when she realized she had no control over Joey and that her marriage was falling apart as a result of the strain.

What went wrong here? While there were many psychological factors at work in this dysfunctional family, we can pinpoint specific actions on the part of the parents that contributed to Joey's negative behavior. The best time for professional help would have been when Joey was in kindergarten: a child and a marriage could have been saved. Joey learned to deal with people in an angry manner by modeling his parents' behavior. Additionally,

Mr. and Mrs. J. always came to Joey's rescue. *Joey never learned that there were consequences for his behavior.*

Consequences are necessary for social development. It was important that Joey be excluded from the class trip when he had broken school rules. He needed to receive poor grades when he didn't do his homework. Mr. and Mrs. J. failed to use these opportunities to teach their son valuable lessons. Joey was never helped to see his role in provoking other children. Mrs. J. sadly exclaimed, "I always believed him. I always defended him. That was my mistake."

It is important for parents to seek out all sides of a story and be open to other points of view. If your child is in the wrong, help him understand the actions that caused others to react the way they did. Role-play other ways of dealing with difficult situations. If your child is always picked on, explore the reasons with your child's teacher. Often, children invite teasing in subtle ways; they might lack social skills and make inappropriate gestures or remarks, or they might misread body language. Encourage your child to build a circle of friends by inviting children to your home. Social skills are learned and need to be practiced. As parents, we must help our children see how others view them and offer alternative ways of behaving.

Dear Dad: What Children Need from Their Dads

Fathers provide a model of how to be a nurturing parent and a caring husband. By a father's example, children learn some of the most important lessons of their young lives—lessons that affect their view of themselves and impact their future relationships with lovers, spouses, and children. A child's relationship with his/her father changes with the passage of time, and with each stage comes a new challenge.

There are times when Father will be favored, and there are times when Father will be rejected. In *Child Behavior,* by Ilg and Ames, the evolving relationship is explored:

> At three-and-a-half in many, there is a change from favoring Mother to

showing a great favoritism for Father. Girls may go so far as to propose to their fathers, who may at this time be their idea of utter perfection, and at four . . . father is for many the ultimate authority. It is Mother, not Father, who is the center of the five-year-old's world. The six-year-old is now fighting to be free of his mother. This means, in actual practice, that the worst trouble areas in a six-year-old's day—dressing, eating, and going to bed—can often be gotten through with relative speed and minimum confusion by a patient and even moderately inventive father.

So, as the child's needs change, Father's role diminishes or intensifies. In *Infants Without Families,* Anna Freud and Dorothy Burlingham state: "The infant's emotional relationship to the father begins later in life than to the mother, but certainly from the second year onward, it is an integral part of his or her emotional life."

Fathers, too, have had to adjust to their changing role and new societal expectations. It is for this reason I decided to write an open letter to fathers on behalf of children. Please give it to your husband or significant other for Father's Day.

Dear Dad,

I feel important when you concentrate on what I'm saying to you. It means so much to me when you stop reading the newspaper or watching television and give me your undivided attention. Although my concerns may seem trivial, they are most important to me. Please do not make light of my problems or mistakes by joking or teasing. I do not understand that and come away feeling belittled.

I get confused when you roughhouse with me and get angry when things get out of hand. Last time, I hit you too hard by mistake. I'm too young to understand degrees of things, so it's best not to play rough with me in the first place.

Please come to an agreement with Mommy about rules. You got angry with me when I jumped on the couch after Mommy said I could do it. I don't know what I can and cannot do when you are in disagreement. I don't want to be manipulative, but when limits aren't clear, I try to get away with whatever I can.

It is important to remember that I do not know what is good for me. I need you to set bedtime routines and good eating habits. Although you may feel that you are being a modern parent by allowing me to go to sleep whenever I want to, I only feel loved and secure when there are routines. In fact, it scares me when I'm allowed to make what should be grown-up decisions. I then become very difficult to deal with.

Please don't expect too much of me. It may take me longer than other kids to learn to ride a bike or hit a baseball. What is important is that we spend time together. I also need time to play alone, to read, to think, and to use my imagination. Having too many scheduled activities (sports, scouts, music lessons, etc.) and not enough unstructured time for myself, causes me to misbehave. In order to protect myself, I may tune out, daydream, or make noises, so please set reasonable expectations.

I would love to spend more time with you alone. Let's go for a walk or work on a project together. You have much to teach me. I'd like you to take me to work and show me what you do. I want you to proudly introduce me to your co-workers and take me out to lunch. I'd like you to come to school and meet my friends and teachers. I'd love to hear stories about when you were a little boy. Please share your experiences and feelings with me. It makes me feel close to you.

Help me know how to deal with angry feelings by letting me see you handle your anger appropriately. It will be invaluable to me as I grow into adulthood.

I know you have big dreams for me, but I need to be allowed to find my own way. Be there for support and guidance. That will make me strong. Dad, I need your approval and affection to grow into a caring adult. Praise me often, and give me lots of hugs and kisses. You're the best!

Love,

Your Child

P.S. Happy Father's Day

PARENTING PROBLEMS: QUESTIONS PARENTS ASK

"My eight-year-old is moody."

"My seven-year-old daughter is being taunted."

"My six-and-a-half-year-old told a lie."

"What can I do with a child who nags?"

"Can a child be addicted to Nintendo?"

"My child says, 'I'm sorry' but continues to hit. Why?"

"Is it normal for a five-year-old to hit his parents?"

Problem: My eight-year-old daughter, Karen, is driving me crazy. She's so moody. She's fine when we are out in public, but at home she's impossible. I don't know what I'm going to do with her. I'm hoping it's just a stage.

Response: It is important to remember that children pass through stages of development at different ages. It is the sequence of the stages that is consistent, and therefore it is helpful to look back on your daughter's behavior in order to establish whether or not she is going through a stage.

Additionally, to determine if this is problematic or typical behavior, ask yourself the following questions: Does my daughter seem happy? Does she have friends? Does she do well in school? Do I feel my relationship with her is generally a good one? Have there been any stressful events in our family that need to be addressed?

Even if you determine that her moodiness is typical for her age, it does not mean you ignore unacceptable behavior. Knowing what to expect at a particular stage of development prepares you to deal more effectively with your child.

So, what can we expect from eight-year-olds? First, they believe they can do almost anything. In fact, they may take on more than they can handle and become very frustrated and tearful when they fail at what they are doing. This high energy, followed by frustration, comes across as moodiness.

During stressful times, it is helpful if you remain calm and reassuring. (Emotions can be contagious.) Break down projects into small manageable parts, and help Karen set realistic goals. When your child is moody and sulking, let her know that you are available to talk when she is ready, and then go about your business. Do not try to cajole Karen out of her moodiness.

Problem: My seven-year-old daughter, Kristen, talks a lot about Jodi. It's sort of a love/hate relationship. Jodi is in Kristen's first-grade class. Kristen complains that Jodi bothers her a great deal, especially in the school yard. (Some days Jodi chooses to play with her; other days, she taunts her and plays with Sarah.) We have tried role-playing with Kristen to help her solve this on her own, but she reports to us that "nothing works." Aside from going to Jodi's mother myself (which I think is the very last option!), I'm not sure how I can help Kristen.

Response: This problem involved three bright, lovely children. This was a case where "three" became a crowd. As often happens with young children, an odd number at play often means "one man out." Here, I was able to have the three girls talk to each other and discuss the problem in school. As is often the case, it was not nearly as serious as Kristen reported to her mother, and the girls quickly worked out a better way of playing together.

Mother did the right thing by contacting the teacher before taking any other action. Additionally, she could encourage other friendships and arrange for playdates to enable Kristen to rely less on Jodi and Sarah. *Helping to build a child's circle of friends is the best way to handle conflict like this.*

Problem: My six-and-a-half-year-old falsely told his teacher and his classmates that he had a new baby brother. He gave the baby a name and reported the baby's progress on a daily basis. I received calls and cards of congratulations. I can't tell you how embarrassed I was! Whatever made him do this?

Response: Some children tell lies to magically change their lives for the better. Others do it for attention and recognition or to cover up a wrongdoing. Sometimes, dishonesty seems the only option when faced with the possibility of punishment or spanking.

In this case, John's favorite aunt had recently given birth, and John was enthralled with the new baby. When his pleas for getting his own baby brother were nixed by his parents, John decided to create one of his own.

It is important that parents not try to catch children in a lie. State the reality as you know it, and express an understanding of the content of the lie. Mother could say something like this: "I know you've been telling your friends that you have a new baby brother. You must want one very much. It is important to tell people that the baby is pretend. You don't really have a baby brother. You just wish you did."

Notice that the words *liar* or *lie* are never mentioned. The emphasis is on helping a child distinguish between reality and fantasy. And, in this case, the child is offered a way to save face with his peers.

Following is a typical example of what happens when a young child is caught in a lie:

Lisa was preparing dinner while her infant daughter was in the high chair and her six-year-old son, Andrew, wandered in and out of the bathroom.

Andrew: Ma, something happened. Come here.

Lisa: Not now, Andrew. I'm busy. I'll be there in a few minutes.

Andrew: But you have to come now. (Andrew had emptied an entire can of cleanser into the tub and on the bathroom floor.)

Lisa: (annoyed, walks into the bathroom) Now, *who did this*?

Andrew: I don't know.

Lisa: What do you mean, you don't know?

Andrew: Batman did it.

Lisa: Now, you tell me the truth!

Andrew accused a ghost, Ninja Turtles, etc. The more he tried to protect himself, the angrier his mother became. Lisa started to yell, and Andrew started to cry. This incident would have ended differently had Lisa immediately said, "Andrew, *you* have made a mess! This is how to clean it up, and you are to get to work immediately." The rule is: *if you know the answer, don't ask the question.* Some parents believe that forcing their children to confess is a way of teaching them to tell the truth. Instead, it encourages youngsters to lie in order to protect themselves.

Lying is a problem when it is frequent. Needy children often lie. It is generally indicative of family problems that could benefit from professional help.

Problem: My six-year-old is a nag. If he doesn't get his way, then he repeats his request a hundred times. Last week, he wanted to invite his friend over to play. I explained that I had work to do and that we would have to make it another time. He did not let up pleading, whining, and pestering me. How can I get him to stop?

Response: Children who nag do it because it works. The best way to stop nagging behavior is to make it clear that when you say no, you mean it. If you are consistent and do not give in, this behavior will stop.

Problem: I'm afraid my five-year-old son is addicted to Nintendo. He plays Nintendo for hours and gets angry if I suggest a change of activity. Should I be concerned?

Response: Children who are "hooked" on Nintendo sit in front of the video screen to the exclusion of anything else. They may talk incessantly about playing Nintendo and sometimes even refuse to play with other children. When parents insist upon shutting off the video game, the children often respond with tantrums, sulking, or withdrawn behavior.

You need to be concerned if the following behavior emerges:

1. An unwillingness to participate in other activities

2. Disinterest in friends

3. Disinterest in books, toys, and schoolwork

4. A lack of creativity and imagination

It is important that parents strictly limit the amount of time children play with video or computer games and are prepared to remove access to the video equipment if rules regarding its use are broken.

Problem: My four-year-old pushes and hits other children. First, I reprimand her and then instruct her to say, "I'm sorry." None of it seems to do any good. What am I doing wrong?

Response: You have given me little information to go on, so I'm assuming your daughter is happy and lives in a home where the discipline is consistent and fair. If this is so, then what she needs to learn is what is and what is not acceptable.

It is fine to teach your child good manners, but with young children, words are not enough. An action must follow the reprimand if it is to become a learning experience. It is usually best to remove the child from the scene of the "crime." "I'm sorry" can serve as magic words that allow children to misbehave and then be quickly forgiven.

For instance, a number of years ago, a boy in my kindergarten class hit another child with a block. I told him to leave the block area. "But," he pleaded, "I said I'm sorry."

"I'm glad you said 'I'm sorry,'" I countered, "but you still may not use the blocks today. Blocks are for building—not for hitting other children with."

Remember that just *talking* to young children is not enough to change behavior. Keep your explanations short and then "do something." Here are some examples of "do somethings":

1. Leave the store, park, or friend's house when behavior warrants it.

2. Immediately take away a toy that has been used to hurt another child.

3. Remove food that is being thrown.

Do not give children second chances—it teaches them not to take you seriously and also encourages them to be manipulative. If you have been inconsistent in carrying out consequences, then start now, and tell your child firmly that there will be no more second chances. Then stick by your word.

Problem: My five-year-old hits me if he doesn't get his own way. I've tried telling him it's not a nice thing to do. I've punished him; I've hit him. He has embarrassed me by slapping me in front of friends and family. Is this unusual behavior for a five-year-old?

Response: The hitting you describe is a serious issue, and it is important to get help in order stop this behavior. (Children should not hit their parents—ever.). Five-year-olds are typically not aggressive. In fact, five is a time of compliance and cooperation. What I have experienced with children who hit, and have good verbal skills, is the following:

1. Children who hit their parents have often seen one spouse hit the other.

2. Children who hit their parents often have parents who use hitting as their primary method of discipline.

3. Children who hit their parents have family roles that are inappropriate.

4. Children who hit their parents are unhappy, scared children.

5. A parent who allows a child to hit him or her feels, on some level, that the hitting is deserved.

The dynamics of your family need to be explored in order to make change happen. I suggest that you get counseling immediately if your child is hitting you.

When Parents Disagree: Parenting Quiz Included

Are you in agreement with your spouse about how to raise the kids? Take this parenting quiz, and compare answers with your spouse. My purpose for preparing this quiz is to spark discussion of your parenting "style."

Parenting Quiz

1. The first time your child used curse words did you …

   a. get angry and threaten to wash his/her mouth out?

   b. explain that "nice children don't say things like that"?

   c. remain calm, saying that he/she may say those words in the privacy of his/

her bedroom but not in front of other people?

d. other?

2. When your child presents a candy bar to the supermarket cashier without your consent, do you ...

   a. pay for it to avoid a scene?

   b. take it away and deal with the tantrum that follows?

   c. try to make a deal; promise to buy something bigger and better later if he/she will put the candy back?

   d. other?

3. When your child refuses to eat the chicken you prepared for dinner, do you ...

   a. say "this is not a restaurant—eat what's served or go to your room"?

   b. prepare another meal he/she likes?

   c. encourage your child to eat the potatoes and string beans but remain firm—no new dish will be prepared?

d. other?

4. When your child's room is a horrible mess
    do you ...

    a. offer to work together with your child to
        clean it up?

    b. insist your child clean it up "or else"?

    c. clean it up yourself, since it's less of a
        hassle?

    d. other?

5. When your child fights with a brother or
    sister do you ...

    a. intervene immediately?

    b. let them work it out as much as
        possible?

    c. tell them they must love each other and
        never fight?

    d. other?

6. When you are out of patience do you . . .

    a. hit?

b. yell and scream?

c. withdraw and cry?

d. all of the above?

Different Upbringings

If you and your spouse disagree on most of your answers, then your parenting styles are probably incompatible. What complicates matters is that each of you has a different recording in your head. Most of us respond to our children in the same manner our own parents responded to us. How often do you find yourself using the same words your parents used with you—words you swore you would never say to your own children? Spouses who have experienced different styles of parenting often have conflicts over whose way is right. Mothers and fathers who develop a new way, a thoughtful combination of their parenting styles, have better-adjusted children and are happier themselves.

You're to Blame

When John and Terri came to see me, they were quick to blame each other for the difficulty they were having with their two children, Betty, six years old, and Jack, three years old. John complained that the house was a mess, with toys scattered in every room:

> We can't take the children visiting. Terri hasn't taught them any manners. They walk across the sofa with their shoes on and roll their trucks on the cocktail table. Terri sees nothing wrong with their behavior. After a day at work, I need some peace and quiet. Just walking into the house sets my nerves on edge. I grew up in a home that was neat and orderly. My brother and I played in our own room and cleaned up our toys every day.

Terri accused John of being a rigid perfectionist, just like his father:

> John wants the children to be like soldiers and respond to orders on command. He expects the house to be perfect, with everything neat and tidy.

I believe children should be allowed to be children. I find it comforting to have their toys around. My family was happy, chaotic, and filled with love. Our children are difficult because John constantly criticizes them. They're manipulative because they know John and I don't agree on what they should and shouldn't do.

I helped John and Terri see that they were each trying to have their present family mirror their own upbringing. John and Terri needed to find their own style of parenting—a style they could each feel comfortable with—one that would be in the best interests of the children because it would include age-appropriate expectations. It was helpful for them to hear that neither parent was at fault but that a new way had to be negotiated. It took several months of parenting discussions before the "John and Terri Parenting Program" was successfully launched.

What to Do When You Disagree with Your Spouse about Parenting

1. Acknowledge your different "styles," and discuss your own upbringing.

2. Each of you should make a list of specific behaviors that you feel are important to foster in your children.

3. Discuss your list with each other, explaining why each item is important to you.

4. Begin statements with "I feel." Avoid attacking—nothing is gained. An example might be as follows: "I feel it's important that Billy eat with us at dinnertime and not be allowed to watch TV. Mealtime is usually a time for the family to be together, and it means a great deal to me to continue that."

5. Listen to your partner, and rephrase what he/she says until your spouse feels understood.

6. Stick to the issue at hand. Do not bring up past grievances.

7. Consider all the options, and work out a compromise. Learn as much as you can about what is age-appropriate behavior and how to set limits in a positive way.

Remember that what matters is *how* you reach your new parenting style. Concern yourself with the process.

PART 2:

IN SCHOOL

TALKING TO YOUR CHILD'S TEACHER

The purpose of this chapter is to help you make your next parent–teacher conference more productive than the one I had many years ago with John's mother. John was a kindergarten child who had difficulty learning. His retention was poor, his attention span was not age-appropriate, and he had difficulty relating to other children. I related this to John's mother by first saying that all children have different styles of learning, and they mature at different rates. I suggested that John be assessed by our school team to determine his strengths and weaknesses, so we could help him do better. At the end of our conference, John's mother looked at me with a big, warm smile and said, "He really is a genius, isn't he?"

As illustrated by this incident, both parent and teacher approach the conference with their own agenda and expectations. At best, the parent–teacher conference is an opportunity for you as the parent to gain insight into how your child learns, relates, and behaves in a group of his peers. It is a time, too, for you to share information that will help the teacher work more effectively with your child. Since most parent–teacher conferences are limited in time, it is important for you to go in prepared to deal with the issues that are important to your family. School systems vary in the amount of information provided by the report card. There may be certain areas that you would like clarified.

Answers to the following questions will give you an overview of how your child is doing:

1. Has my child made progress?

Your child entered the class with a unique set of skills. Where was he/she academically in September? What individual growth has the teacher seen? Is your child working up to capacity?

2. Where is Johnny/Susie academically in relation to the rest of the class?

Clients of mine had a son in third grade whom they referred to as a "math whiz." They were shocked when the school suggested he be placed in a special math class for remediation. With help, the parents soon realized they had not really known how to evaluate a third grader's math proficiency. After observing a third grade math class, they concluded that the school was acting in their son's best interest.

Although I believe parents have a right to know their child's class standing, I am sometimes reluctant to give out this information for fear that parents will put undue pressure on their young child. Plus, class standing can seemingly change overnight as a child "breaks the code" and begins reading well.

So, while class standing information will give you a more realistic view of your child's performance, it is important that you use it constructively to build confidence and provide support.

3. What are my child's strengths and weaknesses?

   This will help you determine the subjects where extra assistance at home might be beneficial. In addition, organize activities around the area where your child excels, to build self-confidence and to help him or her make friends.

4. How does Susie get along with others? Who are her friends?

   Children who have good social skills generally do better in school. Fostering friendships by encouraging playdates may be in order.

5. Is Johnny attentive? Can he carry out instructions? Does he approach his work in an organized way? Does he appear confident or fearful?

If any of these areas are problematic, it will impact greatly on your child's performance in school.

Information to Consider Sharing with the Teacher

Ask yourself these questions:

1. Are there any medical issues the teacher should be aware of?

2. Is there anything about your child's personality, learning style, or likes and dislikes that would be helpful for the teacher to know?

3. Has there been a significant event in the family, such as a death, the birth of a new sibling, or a divorce? Has the family recently moved? (Any significant change can greatly affect a child's ability to learn.)

This knowledge helps the teacher to be alert to behavioral changes, to give extra TLC, and to read selected books and have class discussions about the topic.

Most teachers are dedicated, hardworking people who want to do the best job possible, so it is helpful to approach the conference with a positive attitude and a determination to be a good listener. Remember—both you and the teacher want your child to be successful and to enjoy school.

How to Ease a Young Child's Adjustment to School

Jane stood by the kindergarten classroom door, so she could get a glimpse of the children gathering inside. She felt tears well up in her eyes at the thought of saying good-bye. The classroom was on ground level, and Jane walked from window to window to view the activity inside and peek at her five-year-old daughter, Susan.

Separations are difficult for parent and child, and yet they are essential for healthy emotional development. Separating, like most things in life, takes preparation and practice. Young children who have been encouraged to take care of their own needs, such as toileting, dressing, and feeding themselves, feel confident they can manage without Mommy or Daddy and adjust more easily to school.

Sam was a little boy in my kindergarten class who had a difficult time adjusting to school. Sam was a quiet, well-behaved, overweight child who was frequently near tears over the most seemingly insignificant things. He could not dress himself or handle simple classroom routines. He said, "I don't know how," at the beginning of any new task and wanted me to do it for him. Sam needed months of reassurance that nothing terrible would happen if things weren't done just so. After completing a project, he always asked me "am I done?" I would respond, "Do you think you are done?" Sam would sheepishly reply yes.

Sam's mother worked full-time, and his grandmother was raising him. Sam's grandmother did everything for him. She dressed him, she fed him, and she babied him. Sam got the message that he was not capable of taking care of himself. His lack of self-confidence prevented him from enjoying new experiences and caused him to be easily frustrated.

Without realizing it, Sam's grandma wanted to feel needed, and she doted on Sam in a way that prevented him from developing a sense of autonomy. When Grandma became aware of the problems Sam was having in school, she willingly learned how to help him become more independent.

It is important that parents and caretakers have expectations for young children that are appropriate for their age. When expectations are too great, a child is made to feel inadequate. The message to children is that nothing they do is good enough. When expectations are too few (as in Sam's case), children remain dependent and become insecure.

Remember that parenting is a job where the goal is to put yourself out of business (heard through the grapevine—author unknown.)

You can help make your child's transition from home to school easier by doing the following:

Before School Begins

1. Buy clothing that your child can manage. Check for sturdy buttons and zippers. Jeans with elastic waists enable young children to manage bathroom routines easily. Allow your child to dress himself/herself even if it takes a long time. Put name tags on everything.

2. Visit school with your child a few days before opening day. (Do this even if you visited the classroom the previous year.) Familiarize your child with the building. Count windows and doors. Walk around the school yard.

3. Read books about beginning school. Use them as a springboard to discussing feelings.

When School Starts

1. Allow plenty of time, so the morning is not rushed.

2. Be prepared to stay in school if your child is upset. *Never, ever sneak away*. Let your child know when you are leaving and when you will return. (Make sure to inform your boss that you may be late for work, so you do not feel pressured to leave an upset child.)

3. Arrive at the bus stop or school a few minutes before dismissal time. Young children become frightened if they do not immediately see their parents.

At Home

When you ask your child "what did you do in school today?" a typical response is "nothing" or "I don't know." A better way to encourage your child to tell you about his or her day is to talk about all the things you did at home or work and then ask specific rather than general questions. Remember that it is normal for children to say little or nothing about what went on at school—in an effort to separate themselves from their parents.

End the day with a bedtime story, words of praise, and a hug.

Bright Child—Poor Grades

I recently received a phone call from a mother who was upset that her seven-year-old son showed little motivation in school:

> He is a bright child, but he doesn't apply himself. He makes little or no effort, and I don't know what is wrong. His grades are poor, and he doesn't seem to care. What causes a child to behave this way?

I explained that there are varied reasons bright children do poorly in school, and it would take some investigating to find out the cause of his behavior.

This chapter will explore some of the more common reasons why bright children do not do as well as they should in school.

Physical Problems

Susan, a first-grader, looked out the classroom window when she should have been doing her work. Her handwriting and reading were poor. Mrs. S. tried to help Susan but made little progress. Both Mother and daughter were frustrated.

When Mrs. S. brought Susan to see me, I was struck by the child's extensive vocabulary and sense of humor. After further evaluation, it became clear that Susan had all the necessary skills to read.

Even though Susan had had a basic vision test in school, I suggested, as a first step, a complete eye exam by an ophthalmologist. It was discovered that Susan had a vision problem that was easily corrected with glasses. Within a few months, she was functioning at the top of her class. *All children should have a complete vision and hearing evaluation before they begin school.*

Family Stress

Nicole's mother was in the hospital. Ed's grandmother had recently died. Jackie's parents were getting divorced. Brian's father had lost his job. Often, parents are surprised at the emotional impact of tension on young children. *The family functions as a unit, and anything that affects one member of the family affects everyone in the family.* When parents come to see me about a problem child, these are my first questions:

1. Has this always been a problem?

2. If not, when did his/her behavior change?

3. Were there any changes or stressful events taking place in your family at that time?

Sometimes, parents are so overwhelmed by events in their own lives that they cannot give, or may not even recognize the need for, extra emotional support to their children. In many cases, professional help is necessary to prevent school-related problems from developing.

Wrong Grade

Bobby had entered kindergarten at four-and-a-half years old. He was one of the youngest children in his first-grade class and was experiencing difficulties typical of boys his age. Bobby was immature and not ready for the demands of first grade. After I assessed Bobby's physical, emotional, and intellectual development, I assured Bobby's parents that the problem was immaturity, not lack of intelligence. Bobby was bright. His poor school performance was due to grade overplacement.

Children often experience school failure when they are in the wrong grade. Although there is much controversy about whether or not to retain children in a grade, I have found that immature children benefit greatly from repeating a grade. In order to prevent this problem from occurring, many states wisely require children to be fully five years old before they begin kindergarten. If your child has a November or December birthday and is experiencing difficulty in school, an evaluation to ascertain maturational development is in order.

Overprogrammed

This is probably the most common cause of poor school performance of bright, middle and upper-income children with educated parents. Typically, a child will be participating in music and swimming lessons, a variety of sports, religious education studies, dance lessons, and Brownies or Cub Scouts. The child who is overprogrammed is often unable to focus in class. In addition to being overstimulated, he/she is not being allowed the freedom to be a child and to engage in unstructured activities.

Insufficient Sleep

This seems so obvious and yet every year, I see bright children who cannot do their best in school because they are tired. Sleep needs differ for every child, and parents must assess what is right for their child. If your child has difficulty getting up in the morning, then he/she is probably not going to sleep early enough.

Cluttered Environment

Children cannot do their best when their physical environment is chaotic and distracting. (This goes for classrooms as well as bedrooms.) An uncluttered room, with everything in its place, can help your child focus and improve organizational skills. Not too long ago, I tutored a bright seven-year-old in reading. Richy's workspace was a messy desk that the entire family used. The folder I gave him for his completed work could never be found. Practice material was routinely lost. It was no wonder that Richy wasn't working up to his potential. Children need to have their backpacks, books, and pencils easily available in order to do their best work. In addition, homework should be done without the distraction of music, television, or bothersome siblings. When you provide the proper learning environment, you are conveying that schoolwork is important.

Unrealistic Expectations

Mr. and Mrs. L. were concerned about their daughter Laura's fearfulness and reluctance to participate in her second-grade class activities. After I observed the family interaction during a home visit, it became clear that both parents had unreasonably high expectations. Laura's fearfulness came from feeling inadequate. Since she could never please her parents, she gave up trying.

During a parenting session, Mrs. L. described herself as a perfectionist. "I do things quickly and don't have the patience to wait for Laura. But," she added, "I never put her down." I explained to Mr. and Mrs. L. that Laura was getting the message, a nonverbal one, that what she did was never good enough. For example, Laura's mother felt the need to fix her young daughter's art or science projects before they were brought to school. She would adjust lines that hadn't been cut straight, color in empty spaces, or arrange things more attractively on the paper. Mother needed to understand that every correction she made undermined Laura's confidence. Parents have an obligation to support and encourage—not to perform the task.

We talked about the importance of allowing Laura to be imperfect and discussed appropriate expectations for a child her age.

As you can see, there are many possible reasons why children do poorly in school. Remember: it is important to promptly address the cause of poor grades in order to prevent school failure.

IF YOUR CHILD IS GIFTED

Gifted children have innate ability. They create, they invent, they investigate, and they find new and imaginative ways to use materials. Their curiosity seems endless, and so does their ability to assimilate and process new information. Gifted children may excel in one area or many. Primarily, they display talent way beyond their years and present a wonderful challenge to parents and teachers alike.

During my more than thirty years of teaching young children, I have taught many very bright children. Few children, however, were gifted. In order to clarify my definition of "gifted," I will share stories of children who deserve that distinction.

Billy was in my kindergarten class many years ago. He was a delightful, friendly five-year-old who greatly enjoyed participating in class. Early in the year, we made a birthday chart, and I asked children when they would be celebrating their birthdays. A few children gave incorrect dates, one boy shook his head, and another shrugged his shoulders. Billy called out every child's birthday correctly. In fact, he knew the dates for all twenty-eight children! He had taken the class list home and memorized every child's birthday. It quickly became apparent that Billy had a fantastic memory and was a math whiz. On another occasion, Billy watched me do clerical work. It was May, and I had to figure out each child's age in years and months as of the following September. Billy quickly saw the pattern and started figuring out all the ages. During kindergarten nap time, Billy loved to do seventh and eighth grade math. Yes, he really understood it. My colleagues couldn't quite believe it until they saw it for themselves.

John's fund of knowledge, vocabulary, and comprehension were well beyond his five-and-a-half years. In fact, John's classmates frequently did not understand what he was talking about. Once, I was quite glad for their lack of understanding, because some parents certainly would have objected to the subject matter. John's mother had just given birth to a baby boy. John came to school all excited, wearing green operating garb and carrying a stethoscope and latex gloves. He accurately explained the birth process, why his mother needed a cesarean section, and how it was done. It should not surprise you that John was later admitted to an Ivy League college.

Sam, a first-grader, enjoyed our culminating project in the unit about sea animals. He painted his shoe box blue and put in animals and plants that popped out from the background. Sam, on his own, figured out a way to make the whale "swim" across the box by cutting a slit across the top, attaching a tab to the whale, and pulling it across the box. He then took it upon himself to teach other children how to do it. Sam frequently expanded on what we were doing.

Other gifted first-graders included Marcy, who wrote poetry and chapter stories about topics that interested her, and Susan, who through her marvelous art work, enhanced every subject area. All these children were able to function at levels far exceeding what is usual for their particular age.

If Your Child Is Gifted

1. Have your child tested so that you have a realistic view of his/her strengths. Share the information with school personnel. Unfortunately, many schools are geared to test only children who are experiencing difficulty with learning, so be prepared to foot the bill. (Work in your school district to have this changed.)

2. A maximum class size of twenty-two is best for early childhood classes. This insures that your gifted child has the opportunity to offer opinions, to ask and answer questions, and to receive the individual attention all children need to excel. (Class size is the most important factor—after expertise of the teacher—for quality education of all young children.)

3. Socialization is the key to success in school and in later life. Encourage playdates with classmates. Also, seek out other gifted children for your child to interact with.

4. Make sure your child has access to quality enrichment activities in and out of school, such as fully equipped science and computer labs or a multimedia art program. Be selective, however. *Do not overschedule activities.*

5. Investigate all educational options. A private school may happily give your child a scholarship. Remember, too, that local districts are required to provide appropriate education for all children.

6. Foster a love and excitement for learning by being a role model.

7. It is important to resist exposing your child to emotional experiences that are not age-appropriate. Psychologically, your child is young, even if his vocabulary and other skills are advanced.

8. *Allow your gifted child to be a child.*

WHEN YOUR CHILD SAYS "I HAVE NO FRIENDS"

At the beginning of every school year, children worry if they will have friends in their new classes. Some children make friends easily while others take time to develop friendships. Personality, maturation, and experience are determining factors in how your child relates to others. The following are answers to questions I have been asked about this issue.

Q: How should I respond when my six-year-old son tells me another child called him stupid?

A: Young children often call each other names, and it is important that parents not blow a name-calling incident out of proportion. Children model adult behavior, so react calmly. Remind your son that he can do many things well. Help him find the words he needs, and encourage him to go back to the offender to say in a humorous way: "I'm not stupid! I'm smarter than you." Gently assisting your child to find the words to use will help him gain control and feel better. In addition, it sometimes helps to role-play the situation with your child. It's a productive way to help him let out his anger and frustration.

Q: My eight-year-old often complains of being teased in class. I don't know how to help her.

A: You do not mention what your child is being teased about. I know of children who are teased because they smell, and others because they are overweight. Some children are teased for seemingly no reason at all. You need to know what was said to your child in order to plan a course of action.

Speak to your child's teacher. How does your daughter interact with her peers? Is your child doing anything to provoke this behavior? Is your child being teased because she cannot keep up with the work? Is your child overly sensitive? What action can the teacher take to help the situation? I have found that some children who lack social skills do not pick up nonverbal cues in the form of body language and facial expressions, and therefore they misread them and act inappropriately. Adult intervention is often necessary to help children decipher nonverbal language.

Q: My four-and-a-half-year-old is a follower, and her friends are constantly telling her what to do. Whenever they play house, she is always assigned the role of "baby." Her kindergarten teacher observes the same behavior in class. What makes her behave this way? She is a very bright, verbal child.

A: There are several possible reasons for this behavior. In the chapter "Bright Child—Poor Grades," I discussed the effect that overplacement in a grade can have on school performance. Often, girls who are not fully five when they begin kindergarten can handle the routines and academics, but they have difficulties socially. Parents sometimes believe that verbal ability alone is an indication of maturation and are surprised when their daughters have difficulty relating to their older peers. I have seen very bright four-and-a-half-year-olds unable to handle the socially more adept five-year-olds. Remember: a child's capabilities at four-and-a-half and at five years of age are very different.

Your daughter must also deal with children who are almost a year older than she. An evaluation to determine her maturational development would help you decide how to proceed. Another possible cause of this behavior occurs when parents refuse to allow their child to grow up. For example, I had a little girl in my kindergarten class who was literally pulled from one activity to another by children in the class. She never made decisions on her own. She, too, was always the "baby" in the housekeeping area. At our parent–teacher conference, I discovered that she was still drinking from a bottle and was only recently taken out of a crib. It took some doing to convince these parents that their daughter was acting like a baby because she was treated like one. Age-appropriate expectations needed to be set.

And one final response to your question. When did this infantile behavior begin? Is there a new baby in the family? Having a new brother or sister can cause an older sibling to play at being a baby.

Q: My five-year-old son's play often becomes aggressive. Other parents are reluctant to allow their child to visit at our home, and I can't say that I blame them. I've tried explaining, yelling, punishing, and rewarding, but nothing seems to make an impression. What can I do to stop this behavior? I want my son to have friends.

A: It is necessary to find out the cause of his behavior in order to help him socialize in an acceptable way. Here are just a few of the most common reasons children hurt other children:

1. Children who are hit by adults, hit other children.

2. Children who are exposed to aggressive behavior on TV often act it out in real life. For example, one child in my class had other children in a stranglehold whenever

possible. I found out he routinely watched wrestling on TV.

3. Some children behave aggressively when parental demands are too great.

4. Some children behave aggressively when limits have not been set in a consistent, fair way.

5. Sometimes children react to family stress (divorce, death, etc.) by becoming aggressive.

Q: My six-year-old has very few friends. He seems content, but it concerns me. How can I help him foster friendships?

A: I'm not sure what you mean by "very few." Some children are happy with two or three close friends; other children need a crowd. What is more important than the number of friends your child has, is the quality of the relationships and if your child appears happy and is doing well in school. The following are some general suggestions for helping children to develop and maintain friendships:

1. Help your child develop an interest or skill to excel in. Encourage him to join a group where there are children with similar interests.

2. Invite classmates to your home. All children need a friend from their school classes.

3. Occasionally, take along one of your child's friends on a family outing to the mall or movies.

4. Invite your child's best friend for a sleepover.

5. It is better to invite one child at a time for a playdate. Two young children play better together than three. With an odd number, there is often "one man out."

If you are concerned about how your child relates to others, then discuss it with your child's teacher. Seating arrangements, class projects, and small work groups can all be used to help children build friendships in class.

A New School Year—
Questions Parents Ask
about Educational Issues

"Will my child be bored in
kindergarten?"

"Open classroom or traditional—which
is best?"

"English as a second language
kindergarten—does it work?"

This chapter will answer questions on specific
educational issues that have great impact on
how your child learns.

Q: **My daughter is entering kindergarten
this September and is already reading.
She attended an all-day nursery school
that emphasized academics. I'm
concerned she will be bored and am**

considering asking that she be placed in first grade. What is your opinion?

A: It is not uncommon for children to enter kindergarten reading. Kindergarten is geared to accommodate children with a wide range of abilities. Your daughter, like all children, may develop unevenly. A child can be reading but be less advanced socially or have math concepts that are way ahead of language development. Sometimes, a child's physical maturation lags behind cognitive development. An extreme example of how a child's development can vary happened many years ago in my kindergarten class. Five-year-old Billy was able to do seventh and eighth grade math, yet his verbal and social skills were that of a younger child. *A good kindergarten program will take your daughter from where she is and help her progress in a way that is best suited to her individual needs.*

In addition, your daughter will use classroom materials differently than she did in nursery school and will expand her knowledge in the process. For example, she can exercise greater math ability, organizational, and perceptive skills and build more complicated structures when playing with blocks. In addition to using the educational materials in a more mature way, she will have the opportunity to use her reading ability to write stories and read them in class.

During the course of my teaching career, several parents have insisted on placing their kindergarten age child in first-grade, and it *always* put the child at a disadvantage. It has been my experience that bright children are never bored when they are in a rich environment. Instead, they create, invent, and discover. *Remember that you can't make a five-year-old into a six-year-old.* Maturation takes time.

Q: Do children do better in an "open classroom" or in a more structured environment?

A: In an open classroom (which is no longer in fashion), children work in small groups in centers of learning around the room. At any given time, groups of children may be working at a science, math, or art center. Children usually move from center to center and do not have their own desks. More structured classrooms may have a few or even many centers around the periphery of the room. The teacher usually teaches basic skills to the whole class and breaks the students up into small groups for reading or specific needs. Children do most of their work sitting at their own desks. Cooperative learning, where children help each other, is incorporated into the program. Very traditional classrooms still exist, and my niece, until recently, attended one. Her teacher taught lessons, including reading, to the entire class. The class was never divided for instruction, and the children were given lots of worksheets to keep busy. The school administration believed that the small classes and homogeneous population made group instruction unnecessary. In my opinion, respect for individual differences and the fostering of creativity and reasoning skills were severely lacking in this traditional classroom.

The success of any teaching situation depends on these factors:

1. Number of children in the class

2. Number of discipline problems in the class

3. Availability of teaching materials and support services

4. Teacher training and comfort level with the type of instruction

5. Teacher experience—the more, the better

6. Knowledgeable and supportive administrators

So, the answer to your question is, "It depends," but, in my opinion, more children are successful in a semi-structured setting than in the open classroom. The increased noise level and movement that is a feature of the open classroom is very distracting for many children. At risk is any child who has difficulty focusing or who lacks self-control. The younger, immature child may also suffer in this situation. As is so often the case in education, something is either in or out of vogue. No one way of teaching works for every child, so I prefer to incorporate the best of all methods and styles into my classroom.

If you need to decide on the best placement for your child, then take into account your child's temperament, attention span, social skills, and general maturation.

Q: My family speaks Korean at home, and my son has been placed in an English as a Second Language (ESL) kindergarten class. Is this the best place for him to be?

A: The answer to your question is an unequivocal no. An ESL kindergarten is made up entirely of Non-English (NE) children or those with limited English proficiency. The instruction is in English.

Children learn English best from interacting with English-speaking children, and kindergarten is the ideal place for this to happen. Non-English speaking children can follow their classmates when their teacher gives instructions and have many opportunities to speak with their peers. After spending less than six months in a regular kindergarten class, NE children are usually speaking English and socializing. By the end of the year, they are fully integrated into the classroom setting. In my experience, this is not so with children who have been in an ESL kindergarten. Although they have learned enough vocabulary to test out of the ESL program, they are hesitant to socialize with English-speaking peers, do not follow directions as well, and generally progress at a slower rate in first grade than children who were in a regular kindergarten class.

A New School Year: Questions Parents Ask about Adjustment to School

The beginning of school is a stressful time for both children and parents. This chapter will answer some of the most frequently asked questions concerning school adjustment.

Q: Although my child attended nursery school for two years, he is anxious about beginning kindergarten and is eating and sleeping poorly. Is this typical behavior? I expected an easier transition.

A: The answer depends on the degree of your son's anxiety. Many children exhibit nervousness as the first day of school approaches, and what you describe is most likely typical behavior. The prospect of meeting a new teacher and new classmates in unfamiliar surroundings is difficult for children of all ages. *It is important to acknowledge your son's feelings without expressing disappointment in his behavior.* In addition, follow the suggestions at the end of this chapter.

Q: I'm upset because my daughter was put into a second grade class with none of her friends. The principal refused to rectify the situation, because he believed this was the best placement for her. I'm worried that she will be unhappy, and her schoolwork will suffer. Are my concerns justified?

A: Although I understand your concern, the more accepting you are of the situation, the easier it will be for your daughter to adjust. Children quickly pick up on their parents' attitudes and act accordingly. Most children make new friends quickly, and you can speed up the process by inviting a classmate to your home as soon as possible.

Q: I'm surprised at how ambivalent I feel about sending my son off to school for the first time and find myself worrying

about how he will manage without me.
I realize my fears are unjustified, but
I'm having a hard time "letting go."
My husband tells me I'm being overly
protective. Am I?

A: Separations are difficult for parent and
child, and yet they are essential for healthy
emotional development. Separating, like
most things in life, takes preparation and
practice. It is important that you convey a
feeling of confidence in your son's ability to
manage, so he can go off to school happily.
Many parents feel anxious when they first
leave their child in the care of another adult.
Discuss your feelings with a close friend
or relative who can be supportive. Talk to
other parents who are going through the
same thing. They are easy to find; they are
peeking in the classroom windows!

Q: For the first three days of kindergarten,
my daughter will be attending school
for just one hour. Parents are required
to be available during those three days.
My daughter has been in day care since
infancy, and I wonder if this slow
transition is really necessary?

A: Yes. It makes parents and children feel comfortable with new routines and allows for a smooth start to the school year. When I taught kindergarten, I always asked parents to stay for the first day, and then I decreased their time in the room, by Day Three, to ten minutes. I did this as much to benefit the parents as the children. The parents' positive feelings impacted on their children. As a result, the children in my kindergarten class had fewer separation problems.

DEAR TEACHER

During the course of my teaching career, I have received many letters from parents, expressing a variety of concerns. Hopefully, my response to a few of these letters, from kindergarten and first-grade parents, will help you gain insight into your own child's behavior and help you deal with your child more effectively. The following are actual letters; only the names have been changed.

Dear Ms. Griffin,

I would appreciate it if you would allow my daughter Susan a few minutes to explain a situation involving Betty, which happened in school yesterday. This situation has been causing Susan's disturbance for the past few weeks. I explained to you that I am a widow with another small child, and I have no help. Please advise me as to what is really happening and how to handle it. I am calling the school office, and I would like Betty's home phone number so I can speak directly to her mother.

I trust my daughter completely and, from what she explains to me, Betty always singles her out. "I can beat the hell out of you" is what Betty has said to Susan more than once. Please help me if you can.

Susan and her family were under a great deal of stress. Susan was dealing with the death of her father and the resultant loss of her mother's time and affection. In order to get attention at home, Susan complained about the nicest child in our class. When I brought Susan and Betty together to discuss the problem, Susan just shrugged her shoulders and said, "There is no problem." Susan liked Betty, as did all the other children in the class. The reports of verbal harassment were reserved for Susan's mother alone.

I suggested that Mother respond calmly to Susan's accusations by encouraging Susan to inform the teacher when Betty was bothering her. Also, Susan needed extra, positive attention both at home and in school. As soon as Mother stepped back from this issue, Susan's complaints ceased. In addition, Susan's family needed professional help to cope with the crisis in their lives.

Dear Ms. Griffin,

I am writing this letter for my son John. My son vomits after he eats. I have taken him to doctors, and he had X-ray tests done, but they couldn't find the cause of his problem. He tends to vomit when he eats outside our home and usually at lunchtime. I have been telling him to eat slowly and not to run after he eats. He is afraid to eat in school because he might vomit. Please tell the teachers on duty in the cafeteria that my son can't tolerate eating fast like the other children.

After observing John in class, I was convinced that he was vomiting to fulfill his parents' expectations. They repeatedly stated that John was not like other children his age, and they would go through a list of behaviors they believed were atypical. John did his best to prove them right. Although his parents thought of him as "different," John's behavior (aside from the vomiting) was classic for a five-year-old. I instructed the lunchroom teacher to ignore John. She was not to comment on what or how much he ate. John was to be treated like the other kindergarten children and allowed to play in the school yard without restriction following his meal. John was a good eater and *never* vomited in school. Once John's parents set appropriate expectations for their son, we were able to work out a plan to stop John's vomiting at home too.

Dear Ms. Griffin,

Billy has mentioned that he cannot hear well from where he is sitting. He has been very apprehensive about going to school, so perhaps it's another excuse. He seems overwhelmed by it all, as I'm sure other children are also (no friends, no one plays with me, none of my friends are in my class, etc.). I hope his attitude will get better as time goes on. Meanwhile, I will make arrangements to have his ears checked.

If you think we can do anything more at home to help, please let us know.

Billy was a bright, social, handsome, verbal child who was very manipulative. When I spoke with Billy's parents, they mentioned that they questioned Billy at length about each school day: "Whom did you play with? Who won't be your friend? Why won't they be your friend? Who was your partner on line?" etc. Billy felt obligated to answer and made up stories as he went along. I suggested that, for a time, the parents not question Billy about school at all. I assured them that if there were a real problem, Billy or I would let them know. After a week or so, I met with Billy's parents again. "You were right," they chuckled. "Billy's problems at school vanished as our interrogation of him stopped."

Dear Ms. Griffin,

Bobby has informed me that he has to bring in five quarters and a toy to school; however, he does not remember what it's for. I would like to be aware of Bobby's school activities, yet he cannot remember verbal instructions. I get home late, and he tends to forget, due to the long day he has had. I would greatly appreciate written instructions as a means of communication between you and me, so I can be involved in my son's education.

Bobby had just been in first-grade three weeks when this letter arrived. He was having difficulty focusing on a task and following directions. His kindergarten teacher believed he was hyperactive and suggested he take medication. (Hyperactivity is the catchall for difficult children.) My view was that he needed structure, not drugs, along with firm, clear, and consistent expectations and lots of praise. It was with this in mind that I sent the following letter to Bobby's mother:

Dear Ms. B,

The purpose of verbal homework is to make Bobby responsible for it. Possibly, he can be instructed to tell his babysitter what the homework is as soon as he leaves school. In this case, the children were asked to bring in five pennies to purchase something in our toy store. I'm certain when he sees the store in operation he will want to participate and bring in the proper coins. In time, Bobby will realize the importance of being a good listener.

Often, parents want to shift the responsibility for homework to me. Children learn responsibility by being allowed to accept the consequences of their behavior and by being praised when they do a good job. In this case, Bobby was completing most of his class work and doing his verbal and written homework by the middle of November. Of course, there were lapses, but Bobby had made much progress and was very proud of it.

Dear Ms. Griffin,

Mary's birthday is Monday. I'm taking the day off and would like to come in and make a little party. What is actually done? How many boys and girls are in the class?

An added piece of information: Mary shares her Dec. 12 birthday with Frank Sinatra—whom she absolutely idolizes. (I know it sounds crazy, but it's true. She has covered her bulletin board with his pictures, goes to sleep with a headset on listening to his tapes—and is driving my husband crazy, insisting that he buy a tuxedo.) As a matter of fact, she wants to stay home from school on Dec. 12 because WNEW is playing twenty-four hours of Sinatra music to honor his birthday. "He's my boy."

He is appearing in Atlantic City this weekend to "celebrate" his birthday. I wrote to the manager of the hotel telling him about Mary being his youngest fan—and they've invited her and a guest to his Friday evening nightclub appearance, so the two can "share" their birthdays together a few days early. They also promised to seat her right up front, so she can see him well.

Picture it—Mary, me, and the big-time, diamond pinkie-ring high rollers!

Anyway, she's ecstatic. After mentioning it to a few close friends and getting blank expressions from them—and having her brother tell her she's weird for liking Frank Sinatra—she has stopped telling anyone about it. But if you ask her about it privately, she'll probably be glad to share the news. Note the blush and the grin! Now, all I have to do is make sure she doesn't fall asleep right up front by 9:30, Friday night!

Homework will be in tomorrow. Drop me a note about arranging Monday's party, please. What time is good?

So, what you are wondering was my response to this letter? "We have twenty-five children in class. Please bring cupcakes, napkins, juice, and cups. Plan to arrive about 1:30 PM. Have a great time Friday night!"

PART 3:

WITH FRIENDS

AND FAMILY

PET PEEVES: WHAT PARENTS DO THAT DRIVE ME AND OTHER ADULTS CRAZY

Observing interactions between other parents and their children can make us aware of our own parenting pitfalls. My observations, and those of my friends, are written in an effort to help you identify—and ultimately curtail—child behavior that is annoying to others. As you read the following examples, remember that social behavior needs to be taught and modeled by the significant adults in a child's life.

Before my parents retired, they owned a greeting card shop. Some parents allowed their children to wander around the store unsupervised, and cards often got bent or dirty. There were times I heard parents say, "Don't touch the cards. The *man* will be angry."

How much better for a child to hear this: "I don't want you to touch the cards. They do not belong to us, and if they get dirty, they cannot be sold." Parents show they are serious when they say, "You need to stay next to me," and take their child's hand. In this way, parents impart their values by teaching children to respect property.

I recently had lunch in a local diner. Two mothers entered with three little girls. As soon as the waiter brought over the booster seats, the three young ladies had a screaming match over which color seat each wanted. The mothers allowed the yelling to go on for several minutes and took no action to stop it. Customers looked at each other and rolled their eyes.

It would have been useful for the parents to escort the children into the waiting area, to discuss proper behavior in a restaurant, and then, after the children calmed down, to return to the dining room. It was the parents' responsibility to use this incident as a "teachable" moment.

A good friend of mine often complains about the behavior of children in church: "Loud children and crying infants make it difficult to concentrate on the service."

It is inconsiderate of adults to allow their children to disturb others in church, theater, or any other adult event. Parents should sit where they can leave easily when their children become restless and disruptive.

The following type of pet peeve ranked high on the list of many parents I talked to:

> Lauren got upset when her friend Mary and her five-year-old daughter, Jill, visited. Jill sat with her shoes on the couch and walked into the living room eating a cookie. Mary made no effort to stop her. Lauren felt uncomfortable setting limits for her friend's child, so she opted to remain silent and upset.

In this case, Lauren had the responsibility for establishing the rules in her home, and it was Mary's responsibility to see that the rules were carried out. In a friendly but firm manner, Lauren could say, "If you want to put your feet up on the couch, let's take off your shoes," and, "In this house, we eat food only in the kitchen." Of course, it is easier for children if rules are consistent, but when that's not the case, children must learn to abide by the rules of the host family.

Sandy's pet peeve was that she could not talk to her friend Michelle on the telephone without Michelle's son Robert constantly interrupting.

> *Michelle and I can't have a conversation without Robert whining about something in the background. Michelle leaves me in the middle of a sentence to talk to Robert. Our relationship is suffering because of this.*

Michelle needs to make it clear to Robert that he is not to talk to her while she is on the phone, and she should set a consequence, like no TV or no playdate, if he does. Additionally, if Robert interrupts the call, Michelle should excuse herself from the conversation and call Sandy back when she is free to talk. Robert should hear the expectation and consequence restated, and then Michelle should make certain the consequence is carried out.

In fact, that is the essence for all these examples: clearly stated expectations and consequences. Of course, parents need to be sure that what they expect and what they set as consequences are appropriate, both to the child's age and to the situation. But equally important is to be consistent and to follow through with the consequence until the child can learn the suitable behavior.

When Children Come to Visit

–

After every holiday, I get calls from friends, family, and clients complaining about visiting children. The person calling me is often feeling hurt, angry, unappreciated, misunderstood, or inadequate as a parent, grandparent, or friend.

The following questions and answers are an attempt to make your holiday gatherings more pleasant for you and your family.

Q: I prepared an elaborate Thanksgiving meal with three different main dishes, two different kinds of stuffing, and a variety of vegetables and delicious homemade bread. My seven-year-old granddaughter Mary announced that she didn't like anything on the table

and wanted to eat leftover pizza from the night before. My daughter, much to my horror, warmed up the pizza and gave it to her. I told my daughter I thought she was spoiling Mary, and she responded by getting very defensive. What do you think?

A: Mary should have been offered a choice of eating what was served or not eating at all. Certainly, there was something on the table—if only two slices of Grandma's homemade bread—that Mary could have enjoyed.

Children need to learn to be appreciative of the work that goes into preparing a meal. In short, they need to be taught good manners.

Q: My grandchildren walk from room to room in my house eating food, and my son and daughter-in-law make no effort to stop them. I always restricted my children's eating to the kitchen. I'm concerned that my new carpeting will be ruined. Should I say anything?

A: Yes! It's your house, and you have a right to establish the rules. Speak to your children, and express your concerns. If your wishes are ignored, then speak directly to your grandchildren and say something like this: "I don't want spills or crumbs on our new carpeting. You need to eat in the kitchen. If you want to walk around the house, I'll save the food for you."

Hopefully, your son and daughter-in-law will support you. If not, be prepared to take food away if the rule is broken. It is important that you not do it in anger but rather in a helpful "I'm saving the food for you" fashion.

Q: My grandchildren, four and six years old, are not required to sit at the table during dinner. Last visit, they crawled on the floor under the dining room table while the adults attempted to eat dinner. Is it unreasonable to expect children of this age to sit and eat with the rest of the family?

A: Young children can be expected to sit at the dinner table until they are finished eating. Children need to be taught that crawling under the dining room table is unacceptable behavior. After they are finished eating, children can be given a "treasure chest" consisting of interesting objects that can keep them busy for long periods of time. The "treasures" can be items like a broken phone, an old camera, discarded jewelry, etc.

Q: I invited several couples for a Saturday night get-together. One couple asked if they could bring their three-year-old son, Brian. They believe in taking him everywhere they go. I reluctantly said okay—and lived to regret it. Brian stayed up until 11:00 PM, and all conversation centered on his antics. When my friends tried to put Brian to sleep, he screamed for a solid hour. How can I prevent this from happening again?

A: There are some parents who refuse to leave their children with a babysitter and never go out as a couple. They believe they are being superior parents by making this sacrifice. Unfortunately, by not doing things as a couple and neglecting their relationship, they are harming their marriage and their child.

Brian's parents can be told that you are looking forward to an evening of adults only. You and your guests have a right to a Saturday night without children. Brian's parents can either choose to get a babysitter or stay home.

Q: I'm upset because I see my grandchildren infrequently. My children are reluctant to visit and recently refused an invitation for Thanksgiving dinner. I know it's my fault, and I want to turn the situation around.

A: This grandmother acknowledged that she often told the couple how to raise their children and was openly critical of their child-rearing practices. She had thought the problem through and decided it might be helpful if she asked them to put aside what had happened in the past and "let bygones be bygones." I responded like this: "That only angers people because it minimizes what happened." It is more productive to say, "I know that I have overstepped my bounds by telling you what to do, and I'm sorry for the hard feelings it has caused. If I start giving unsolicited advice, hold up your hand, so I know to stop. You mean a great deal to me, and I want to work at having a good relationship with you."

The Power of Praise: Its Impact on Adults and Children

When was the last time someone you love said or did something to show his or her appreciation? All of us can recall such moments—or the lack of them—with much emotion. A compliment can keep us going even when times are tough, and, conversely, we feel unloved and unappreciated when praise is not forthcoming. I asked some adults the question posed at the beginning of this chapter. Following is a sampling of their responses:

Women

> "Oh, God, I can't think that far back. It was probably over dinner. It is usually in exchange for a favor. I have to ask for it. Beg for it."

"I'm thinking … Oh, he said I made the cookies better than his mother."

"It's very rare. In forty-two years of marriage, I can count that on one hand."

Men

"I couldn't even answer that. Do people really pay attention to that sort of thing?"

"I have a terrible memory for this sort of thing. Last week she thanked me for cleaning the horse tack."

"Let me think about that. I think you're asking the wrong person."

"We're going through such a traumatic time; we're just keeping the ship afloat."

Appreciation

In my experience, people in happy relationships express appreciation in small ways on a daily basis. For instance, being a stepparent can be very stressful. In the book *Living In Step,* by Ruth Roosevelt and Jeannette Lofas, the authors state the following:

> In almost every instance where we found a gratified stepmother, we have also found a husband who understands, validates, and is simply "there" for his wife as stepmother. Again and again, stepmothers have expressed to us their conviction that, through all their difficulties, the one thing that kept them going was their husbands' appreciation.

The most powerful words are those that convey we are a valued person, that we are loved, that we are special, or that we are a good mother or father. How different our lives would be if we expressed our appreciation to others and heard words of appreciation in return!

Recently, a friend of mine argued that we should not need praise to make us feel good. "If we feel good about ourselves, we don't need to define ourselves by what others say." I countered with this: "You know you do an excellent job at work, but think how happy it made you feel when your boss recently complimented you. And think how you complained when your hard work wasn't recognized. We can have a high regard for ourselves and still need to hear words of appreciation. This is especially true in intimate relationships."

Productive Praise and Children

Children, in particular, thrive on praise and need it to develop self-esteem. Productive praise in conjunction with appropriate consequences fosters social development. Productive praise is specific. It can change behavior by reinforcing what is acceptable behavior. Five-year-old Billy sat at the dinner table without jumping up and down for the first time in weeks. His mother was ecstatic and said, "Billy, you are such a good boy!" A better response would have been: "Billy, you sat at the table until you finished eating. Terrific!" When Billy played nicely with his sister, his father said, "Billy, you are acting so grown-up." Productive praise tells Billy exactly what he did so he can repeat the behavior. "Billy, you shared your toys. That was a nice thing [or grown-up thing] to do."

If you are trying to change your child's behavior, it is important to praise your child *before* he/she has a chance to misbehave. That will encourage the good behavior to continue. For example, when Billy sat quietly at the table for five minutes, praise was in order. Remember, though, praise alone doesn't always work. In addition, children need to know there are consequences for their misbehavior.

In my first-grade class, in addition to verbal praise, I give out "Happy News Telegrams" when children do a good job or are especially helpful. I am specific in the praise that I give: "You did a good job listening today." "Your writing is getting better!" The praise that I give is directly related to behavior. My goal is to have children internalize good behavior, so that eventually behaving in an acceptable fashion becomes satisfying in itself.

Our Little Picasso

So what do you say when your kindergarten child proudly brings home an all-red painting? Parents might respond in one of the following ways: "Oh, it's so pretty." "It's wonderful!" "What a nice picture!"

Here again, praise should be instructive and honest. Children know when you are not telling the truth. A response that helps with concept development, delivered in a pleasant, loving voice would be as follows: "You made an all-red painting," or, "You covered the entire paper and didn't leave any spaces." If it is obvious that your child worked hard on a project, even if the outcome isn't very good, you can say: "That must have taken you a long time to do. Looks like you worked hard on that one."

The good news is that you can start today to improve your relationships by simply letting those close to you, both children and adults, know how much you appreciate them. It takes little effort, costs nothing, and the rewards can be significant. Praise is powerful, indeed!

REMARRIAGE AND CHILDREN

When holidays and personal celebrations are approaching, we think of love and possibly remarriage. In general, census data state that the majority of divorced men and women remarry within four years, and 60 percent of them already have children.

This chapter explores one of the more common myths surrounding remarriage and stepparenting—the belief that the new family can function with the same roles, rules, and feelings as the family of origin.

When Susan and Jim came to speak to me, they were both upset that, since Jim's eight-year-old son, Billy, had come to live with them, their relationship had deteriorated. Susan wanted to be a good wife and stepmother, but she felt used and unappreciated. Billy was difficult to deal with. He often reminded her she was not his mother and couldn't tell him what to do. He was having problems in school and often got into trouble with his peers; his teacher was calling with frequent complaints. Both Jim and Susan agreed that Billy needed more supervision.

Susan made an appointment to see me after Jim suggested that she quit a job that she loved in Manhattan. Jim wanted her to find another job closer to home, so she could be home when Billy returned from school. Jim could see nothing wrong with his request and was surprised by the intensity of Susan's reaction. He earned more money than Susan, and he did not want to risk leaving a good job. More importantly, he saw Susan as the "mother" and expected her to fulfill his view of that role. Susan was the one who took off early from work to attend parent–teacher conferences, and she was the one who usually helped Billy with homework. Jim's request that she change jobs was the last straw.

Jim and Susan both came from traditional families and had no role model for their new family. They needed to renegotiate roles, and Jim's dream of a traditional family had to be replaced by more realistic expectations. Susan was not Billy's mother. In fact, as soon as she backed off from the "mother" role and took on the role of a caring adult, her relationship with Billy improved. Jim took over the parenting role, and Susan supported him. Jim hired an older woman to stay with Billy until they both came home from work. Susan learned to respond to Billy's negative comments, such as "my mother's chicken tastes better than this," by looking for the meaning beyond the words. I suggested, for example, that she respond to Billy's comment by asking him to get his mother's chicken recipe, so they could make it together. The more Susan acknowledged the existence of Billy's mother, the less Billy had to prove his loyalty to her. Once Susan was able to empathize with Billy's pain, she could stop feeling rejected and respond to his put-downs in a light, sometimes humorous way. When her response changed, so did Billy's behavior. Jim and Susan were open to making the necessary changes to strengthen their relationship. As their marriage grew stronger, their stepfamily grew stronger too.

Charles and Barbara lived with Barbara's three-year-old daughter, Nicole. Charles complained that he could not have a discussion with Barbara without Nicole interrupting them. She would whine, cry, have a tantrum, or pull on Barbara's clothes. Charles felt Nicole was "spoiled" and that a good spanking would "straighten Nicole out." Barbara felt Charles expected too much from a three-year-old, and she resented any criticism about her parenting style.

The problem presented here is not unique to stepfamilies, but the stepfamily's way of dealing with it is unique. Both Charles and Barbara needed to learn what is acceptable behavior for a three-year-old and how to set limits without spanking. In a parenting session, we discussed priorities and worked out a plan to change Nicole's behavior. Charles felt "heard" and had a great deal of input into our discussions, but it was Barbara who was responsible for implementing the plan. Charles needed to take a backseat, for a while at least, and concentrate on building a relationship with Nicole. He took Nicole on walks and short trips to the store. As soon as Nicole began to accept him, he took over reading the bedtime story. Nicole's behavior started to improve, with consistency and love. Charles and Barbara learned that establishing warm, trusting relationships within a stepfamily takes effort and patience.

Richard and Karen came to see me with a "small problem." This recently married couple had requested that Karen's six-year-old daughter, Heather, call Richard "Dad." "No way," screamed Heather. "You're not my dad." Richard felt hurt and angry. He was providing Heather with a lovely home so she could attend a good school. Heather's father didn't even pay child support. Karen just wanted a "family" and tried to keep the peace, although lately it wasn't working. In our first session, Richard talked about his feelings of rejection and his desire to have a "real family." Karen wanted that also, but she felt caught in the middle between two people she loved.

We explored the many reasons Heather had for refusing to call Richard "Dad." Here are just a few of them:

1. She had a father.

2. She felt disloyal to her father by calling Richard "Dad."

3. Her relationship with Richard was not well established.

4. She saw Richard as a threat to her relationship with her mother.

5. She was angry over the divorce and wished her parents would get back together.

Once Richard could see it from Heather's point of view, he was able to role-play during our session what he would say to Heather:

> "I realize how difficult it is that your parents divorced and how much you miss your father. It's not easy to call someone else 'Dad.' You can call me by my first name if you like, or 'Stepdad.'

This was the turning point in Richard and Heather's relationship. The level of conflict in their home was greatly reduced.

Stepparenting Wisdom in Brief

1. Building a new family takes time. There is no instant love—but respect is always in order.

2. Remember that every member of a stepfamily has experienced a loss. Be gentle with each other.

3. Create your own family traditions.

4. When a stepchild says something hurtful, respond to the meaning beyond the words.

5. It is best if the stepparent can support the natural parent in matters of discipline.

6. Children in stepfamilies gain strength from a solid marriage.

Stepfamilies are different from traditional families and can't be judged by the same criteria. Expectations need to be adjusted, and the complexity of relationships need to be acknowledged and supported.

PART 4:

AND FINALLY

THE DIFFICULT PARENT:
A GUIDE FOR CHILDREN

As a child, it is helpful to know if you live with a difficult parent. Identifying and labeling your parent as difficult is the first step to making things better at home. Once you have established that you are living with a difficult parent, you can alter the way you react to his or her behavior and thereby change the dynamics of your family for the better. Difficult parents pass through a variety of ages and stages. Knowing what to expect will help you pass through childhood with less trauma.

Young, Inexperienced Parent (YIP)

Having a YIP for a parent requires a great deal of patience and understanding. As a rule, YIPS are nervous and unsure of themselves. Remember that you are his or her first child.

Help build your parent's self-confidence by smiling a lot and behaving well in front of friends and family. When your YIP asks you to sing a song, touch your nose, or show your belly button, don't be offended. The YIP just wants to show relatives how smart you are, which is directly related to how smart he or she is. It is particularly important to sleep through the night as soon as you are physically able. Nothing is worse than a tired, grouchy YIP.

Bright Older Parent (BOP)

The BOP is particularly hard to deal with. A BOP will read every child-rearing theory and try it out on you. The BOP is often a perfectionist and expects you to be perfect too. It's tough to live up to the expectations of a BOP.

When you get to be five or six years old, the problems get worse. The BOP will program your every move if you do not assert yourself early on. You will be scheduled to take dance, music, art, gymnastics, and ice-skating lessons all at the same time. Misbehaving before, during, or after the lesson is often the only way to get some unstructured time for yourself. The BOP tends to talk too much. If you do something wrong, he or she will go on about it for hours.

They explain, explain, explain. Remember that BOPs mean well. Protect yourself by tuning out, daydreaming, making noises, or walking away. Hopefully, your BOP will get the message.

Tired, Industrious Parent (TIP)

Your mom and dad are both working, and they feel guilty about being away from you all day. They are determined to give you quality time. They want to interact with you in a meaningful, thoughtful, educational, creative, dynamic way. Decide on your own whether you are willing to give them what they need. If not, you can quickly put an end to quality time by running and screaming around the house as soon as they come home, refusing to eat dinner, or having a tantrum when it's time to go to bed. Your TIPs will be upset with you, but at least you won't have to deal with quality time.

Smothering, Affectionate Parent (SAP)

The SAP waited a long time to have a baby, and now that you have arrived, he or she does not want you to grow up. The SAP will talk to you in high-pitched voices and spoon feed you until you are four. The SAP will also keep you in diapers or wipe your bottom longer than necessary and let you sleep in the parental bed. Although the attention seems wonderful, you will pay a heavy price for it later when you have trouble adjusting to school and the company of peers. Your immature, demanding behavior will cause you much unhappiness. Hopefully, your SAPs will change their expectations of you after the first parent–teacher conference.

How to Deal with a Difficult Parent (DP)

1. Be consistent. Your DP will understand what you want only if you misbehave at the same time, in the same fashion, every day.

2. Reward your DP's good behavior by remembering to go the bathroom without being told, going to sleep after just one story, or eating dinner without throwing food on the floor. As an extra-special treat, don't fight with your brother or sister.

3. Talk with other children who have difficult parents. It helps to know there are other children with similar problems, and you can give each other support.

4. Get some professional counseling. You can learn strategies and interventions to help you cope with your DP.

Lessons Learned: Important Advice for Parents with Children of All Ages

Recently, I met with a couple whom I know casually, and I commented that I couldn't believe my daughter would be celebrating her fortieth birthday. The man looked at me incredulously and said, "What did you expect? We all get older." The woman looked at me knowingly and said, "It's amazing how fast the time goes by." It was after those two very different responses that I decided to explore what I meant when I said "I can't believe it."

I was referring to how much time had passed since I gave birth to Amy and what a joy it had been to watch her grow and mature. It made me reflect on experiences we had shared and how our relationship had flourished over the years.

I'm taking this time to look back and share memories, and the lessons I have learned along the way.

Amy was sitting in her high chair, screaming, and I couldn't figure out what was wrong. Her face turned beet red, and her crying grew louder. Finally, she started tugging her nose. I looked in her nostrils and saw a foreign object stuck in one of them, just out of reach of my fingers. I called the pediatrician who suggested gently pressing from the top of her nose downward. If that didn't work, I was to bring her to the office. Fortunately, a single bead fell out. (To this day, I have no idea where she found the bead.) She immediately started playing and smiling again, but it took me a while to recover.

Lesson: Young children like to stick things in openings.

Amy had a favorite stuffed animal that my mother and father had given her for a present. She named the rabbit Mitsy and took her everywhere. Soon, Mitsy was very dirty, and I suggested washing her in the washing machine. Amy was agreeable. Poor Mitsy came out of the washer minus one eye and with her head slightly misshapen. I will never forget the look on Amy's face when she saw Mitsy. She sobbed as she held her beloved stuffed animal. I felt awful as I tried to console her. At first, I offered to sew the eye back on, not realizing I would not be able to find it. My parents offered to buy Amy another stuffed animal, but Amy wanted only Mitsy Mayflower.

Lesson: Don't put your child's favorite stuffed animal in the washing machine.

I remember sitting in the hallway with a group of parents while our children were in a classroom being evaluated for acceptance into a prestigious preschool program. The parents were tense; nobody spoke during that critical hour. Finally, the classroom door burst open, and out ran an enthusiastic group of four-year-olds. I waited patiently but did not see my Amy. The classroom door closed again, but Amy was nowhere to be seen. I walked over to the door and poked my head in. "Oh," exclaimed the teacher. "Amy was engaged in water play, and there was much water on the floor. She'll be out as soon as she cleans it up." As I walked back to my seat, all eyes were on me. I could almost feel the pity of the other parents as they contemplated Amy's rejection notice. When Amy came out of the classroom, she was as happy as could be and gave a big good-bye to the teacher. She had had a wonderful time. Yes, Amy was accepted into the program.

Lesson: Preschool and colleges do not have the same standards for admission.

When Amy was nine years old, she went to sleep-away camp for the first time. Oh, how I dreaded going to the mailbox those first few weeks. Every letter was a horror story. There were bats flying around the bunk. The food was awful. It rained in the bunk. She walked to the bathroom with a flashlight during a storm and got all wet, etc. And she wanted to come home. After the initial separation anxiety abated, however, she began to enjoy camp. It took me some time, though, to open one of her camp letters without my heart pounding.

Lesson: If letters from camp are anything less than awful, consider yourself fortunate.

I taught Amy how to drive. I wanted her to get as much experience as possible, so I let her drive whenever we were together in the car. I remember instructing her as follows: "If I tell you to do something, just do it." She drove our old Caprice Classic, so when she scraped the side of it on the stone wall of our driveway, and when she backed it into a fire hydrant, the bangs and dents didn't upset me. I was concerned about her safety and that of her passengers. I must confess, I prayed that Amy would fail her driving test. No such luck—she passed the first time. I'll never forget how nervous I was when she took the car out alone for the first time. My condolences go out to any parent who must yet see their child through this rite of passage into adulthood.

Lesson: Don't give up your old car just yet.

Another milestone occurred when Amy went off to college. I can picture our pickup truck loaded with her personal belongings as we drove her to the dorm. On our journey back home, I started to cry. "Are you okay?" my husband asked.

"I'm fine," I whispered. With that, he pulled the truck over to the side of the road and held me. "Life is full of big and little separations," I said.

It was thrilling to see her graduate from Geneseo and then New York University graduate school as a speech-language pathologist.

Lesson: Separations are always difficult.

And so I say with great pride, "I can't believe it."

CONCLUSION

Every parent needs help from time to time. Some children *are* more difficult than others. Their personalities or temperaments may require an approach or style that is different from what you do naturally. Additionally, negative outside influences and less available family support adds to the pressures of being a parent.

The information and examples in this book will serve to make you aware of the causes of common behavioral problems. Use your new knowledge to prevent difficult behavior from starting, and use the suggestions in each chapter to help fix existing problems.

Follow the advice in this book, keeping in mind that the only way to change your child's behavior is to change your response to that behavior. Therefore, doing more of the same—more yelling, more punishing, more threatening—will not produce change. Think carefully about the issues discussed in the chapters "Bonding versus Crazy Glue" and "What Children Can't Tell You." Review those parts of the book that address problems that are similar to yours. Set priorities, and tackle one problem at a time. For example, if bedtime is a nightmare, then work on improving that first. Your child will put you to the test, so expect behavior to initially get worse. After all, you always caved in before. If you carefully follow the steps for setting limits, then improvement should be evident in about two weeks. At that time, you can deal with another issue.

It is very important that you strictly adhere to the rules and consequences that you establish; there can be no exceptions made. Most parents are surprised at how relatively easy it is to gain back control once they commit themselves to making changes.

Always keep in mind the following:

1. **All children want to be good.**

Remember that children want your love and approval, so when misbehavior is disruptive to family life or causes parents and children undue stress, it's time to take action. Refer to the chapters "What Children Can't Tell You" and "Setting Limits." If the problem is school-related, reread Part 2, and make an appointment with your child's teacher.

2. The purpose of discipline is to teach children what is acceptable behavior.

Most people think of discipline as punishment. I prefer to think of discipline as a way to teach children what is expected. Teaching what is acceptable behavior does not need to be punitive.

3. Clear expectations make children feel secure.

Clear expectations help children do the right thing. I remember one parent who told her son he was acting silly every time he misbehaved. This child had no idea, nor did I, what he had to do to make his behavior acceptable. Although he wanted his mother's approval, he did not know what to do to get it. Remember to be specific in your expectations by clearly stating what you *want* your child to do.

4. Children need and want routines.

Children love routines. They thrive on them. Think of ways you can make old routines work more smoothly. Invent new routines to ease stressful times of the day. Have a family meeting to plan, adjust, and create routines that will help the family function in a happy, productive way.

5. Praise and consequences work best if used together.

Be specific and generous with praise. Keep track of how often you praise your child. It should be a minimum of several times a day. That, in addition to appropriate consequences, will go a long way in creating a positive climate at home.

6. Parents must support each other if discipline is to be successful.

Children will become manipulative and unpleasant company if they are allowed to play one adult against the other. Follow the suggestions in "When Parents Disagree." If you are still unable to reach agreement about matters of discipline, it's time to seek professional help.

7. **Consistency is the key to implementing a change in behavior and, ultimately, to getting your child to listen.**

   Nothing is more confusing for a child than dealing with rules that change often. Rules will more likely be stable if parents agree on them beforehand and if they are fair and enforceable.

It takes time and effort to bring about positive changes, but it is well worth it. Remember that you have the power and knowledge to make things better. Go to it!

BIBLIOGRAPHY

Freud, Anna, and Dorothy Burlingham. *Infants Without Families: Reports on the Hampstead Families.* Madison, CT: International University Press, 1993.

Ilg, Frances, and Louise Bates Ames. *Child Behavior.* New York: Harper Row 1992.

Roosevelt, Ruth, and Jeannette Lofas. *Living In Step.* Columbus, OH: McGraw-Hill, 1977.

Viorst, Judith. *Necessary Losses.* New York: Ballantine Books, 1986.

Made in the USA